MONEY
MOON
MUMMY
MUSIC
MYTHOLOGY
NASCAR
NATURAL DISASTERS
NORTH AMERICAN INDIAN
OIL
OLYMPICS
PERSPECTIVE
PHOTOGRAPHY
PIRATE
PLANT
POND & RIVER
PRESIDENTS
PYRAMID
RELIGION
RENAISSANCE
REPTILE
RESCUE
ROBOT
ROCKS & MINERALS
RUSSIA
SEASHORE
SHAKESPEARE
SHARK
SHELL
SHIPWRECK
SKELETON
SOCCER
SOLDIER
SPACE EXPLORATION
SPORTS
SPY
SUBMARINE
SUPER BOWL
TECHNOLOGY
TEXAS
TIME & SPACE
TITANIC
TRAIN
TREASURE
TREE
UNIVERSE
VAN GOGH
VIETNAM WAR
VIKING
VOLCANOES & EARTHQUAKES
VOTE
WATER
WATERCOLOR
WEATHER
WHALE
WILD WEST
WITCHES & MAGIC-MAKERS
WORLD SERIES
WORLD WAR I
WORLD WAR II

Eyewitness
MAMMAL

Fruit bat crawling

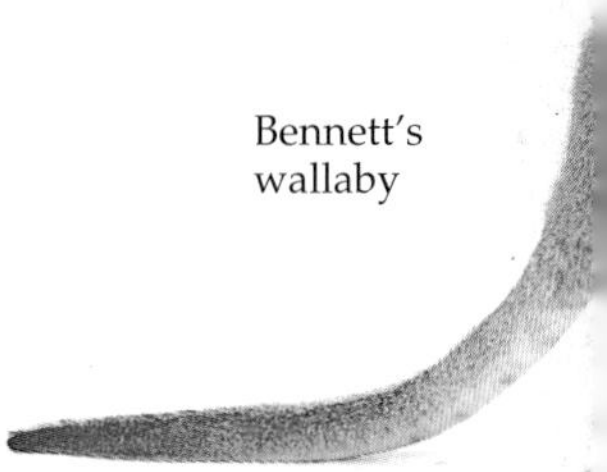

Bennett's wallaby

Hare skeleton

Red fox

Senegal bushbaby

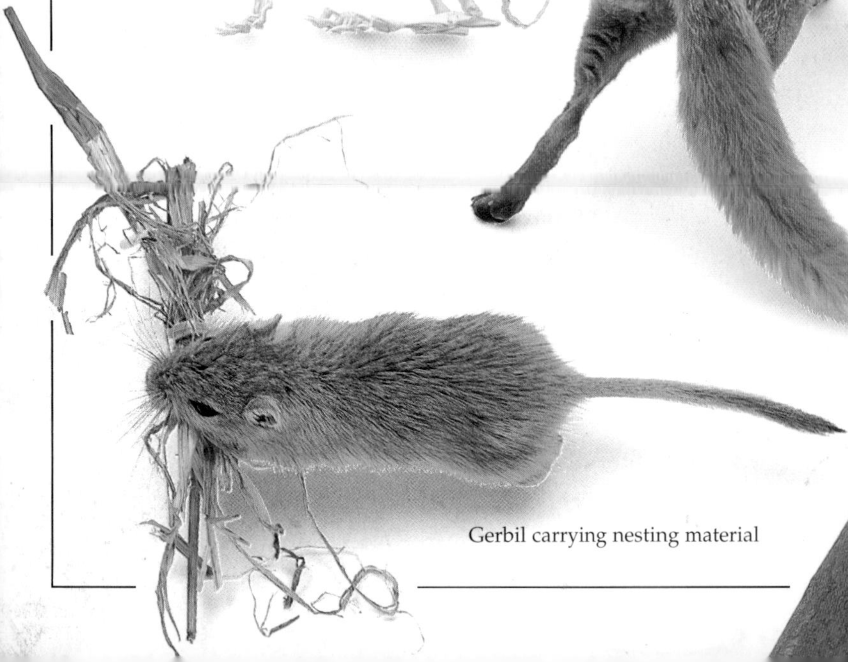

Gerbil carrying nesting material

Hazelnuts opened by dormouse

Eyewitness MAMMAL

Pinecone chewed by squirrel

Written by
STEVE PARKER

Hedgehog about to unroll

Chimpanzee clapping

Hedgehog footprint

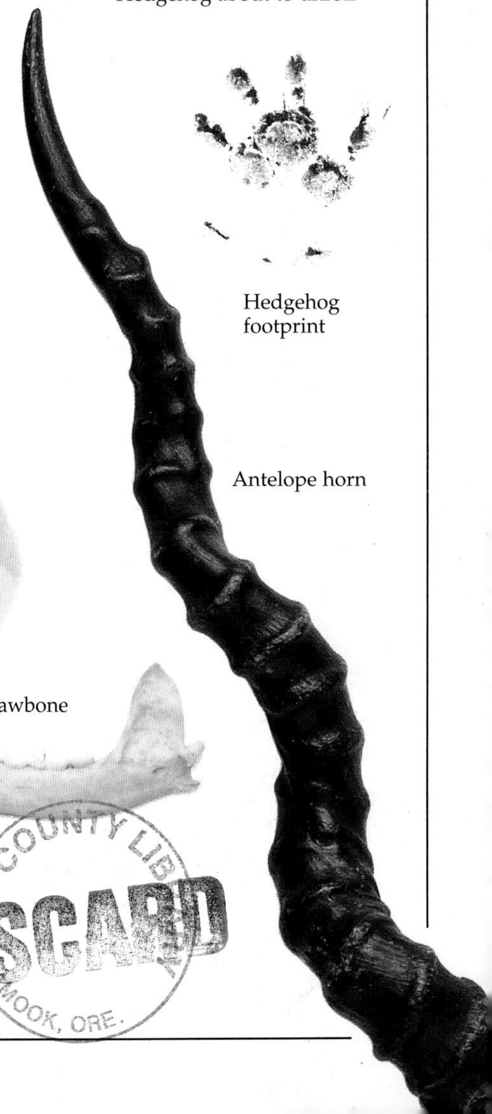

Antelope horn

Puppies playing

Chinchilla eating nuts

Lower jawbone

DK Publishing, Inc.

Domestic cat

Badger rolling

LONDON, NEW YORK, MUNICH,
MELBOURNE, and DELHI

Project editor Sophie Mitchell
Art editor Neville Graham
Managing editor Vicky Davenport
Managing art editor Jane Owen
Special photography
Jane Burton and Kim Taylor,
Dave King and Colin Keates

REVISED EDITION
Managing editor Andrew Macintyre
Managing art editor Jane Thomas
Senior editor Kitty Blount
Senior art editor Martin Wilson
Editor Karen O'Brien
Art editor Ann Cannings
Picture research Lorna Ainger
Production Jenny Jacoby
DTP designer Siu Yin Ho

U.S. editor Elizabeth Hester
Senior editor Beth Sutinis
Art editor Dirk Kaufman
U.S. production Chris Avgerinos
U.S. DTP designer Milos Orlovic

This Eyewitness ® Guide has been conceived by
Dorling Kindersley Limited and Editions Gallimard

This edition published in the United States in 2004
by DK Publishing, Inc., 375 Hudson Street, New York, New York 10014

10 9 8 7 6

A catalog record for this book is available from
the Library of Congress.

ISBN 978-0-7566-0703-6 (PLC) 978-0-7566-0702-9 (ALB)

Color reproduction by Colourscan, Singapore
Printed in China by Toppan Printing Co. (Shenzhen), Ltd.

Discover more at

www.dk.com

Baby
wallaby

Lion's tail bob

Rabbit sniffing the air

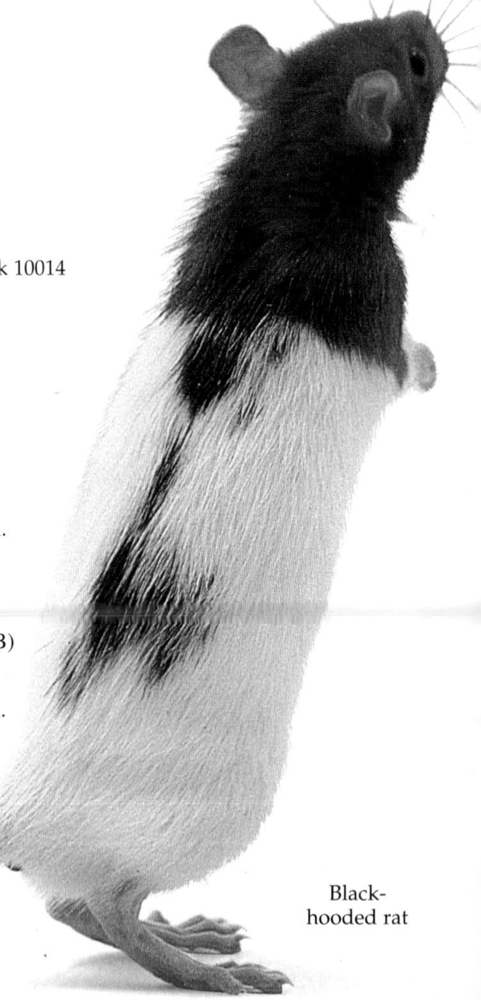

Black-
hooded rat

Contents

Golden hamster carrying baby

The mammal world

HUMANS ARE ONLY ONE of perhaps 10 million different species, or types, of animals in the world. With some animals we may feel uneasy, even though there is no reason: a harmless snake, perhaps, or a slimy snail. Yet others seem to demand our interest. Bush babies, seal cubs, dolphins, kittens, and koalas - we are drawn by their furriness and their warm bodies, and the way the mother looks after her babies. These are things that we recognize in ourselves, and by them we show our membership in the mammal group. For, however much we raise ourselves above our relatives, the human species is just one of the 4,000 or so mammal species on our planet. So what is a mammal? One, mammals have fur or hair. Many have it all over their bodies; we do too, although it shows the most on our heads. Two, mammals are warm-blooded. A more correct term would be

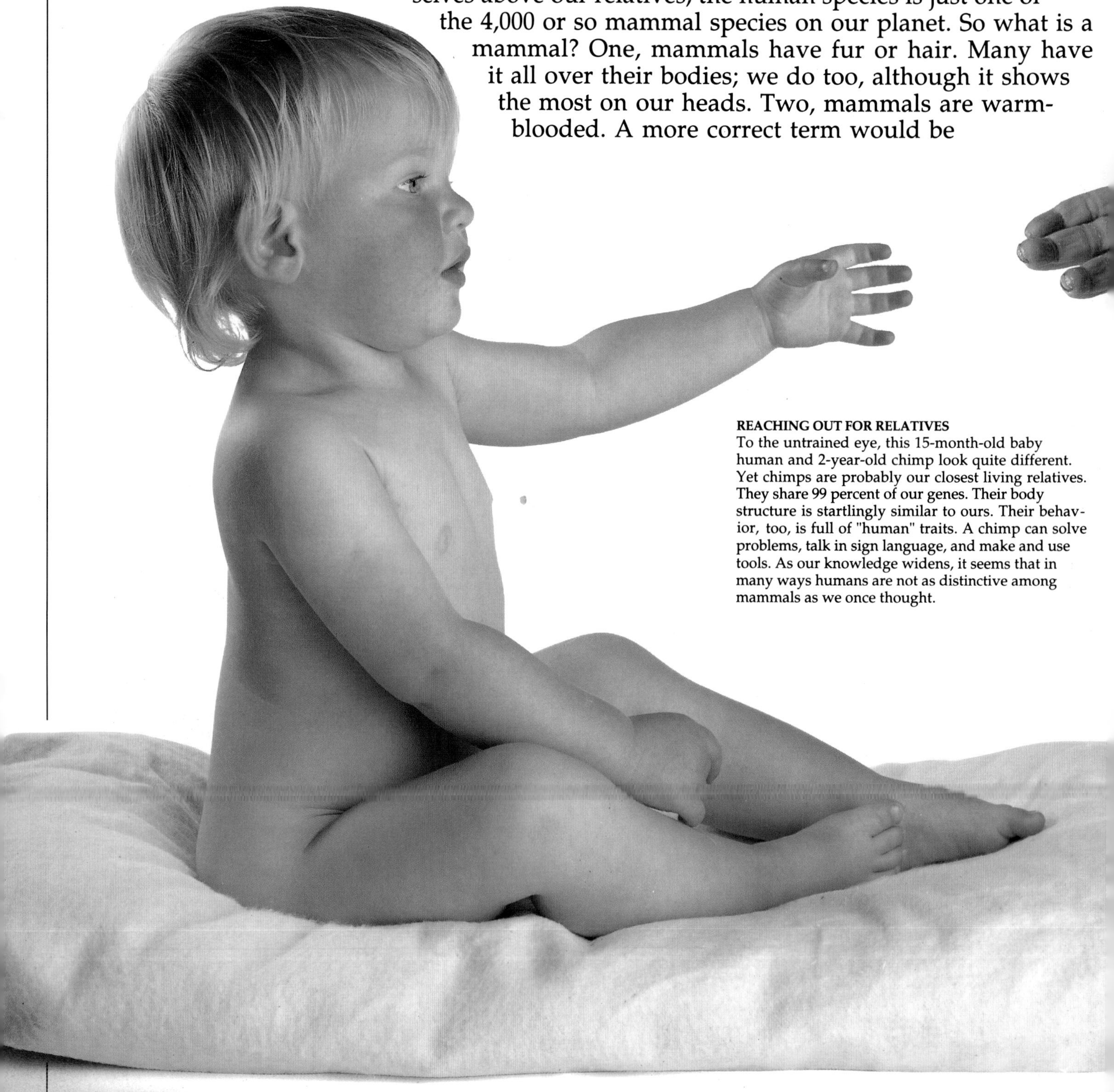

REACHING OUT FOR RELATIVES
To the untrained eye, this 15-month-old baby human and 2-year-old chimp look quite different. Yet chimps are probably our closest living relatives. They share 99 percent of our genes. Their body structure is startlingly similar to ours. Their behavior, too, is full of "human" traits. A chimp can solve problems, talk in sign language, and make and use tools. As our knowledge widens, it seems that in many ways humans are not as distinctive among mammals as we once thought.

homoiothermic, meaning that a constant internal body temperature is maintained, usually above that of the environment, rather than adjusting to the temperature of the surroundings. In this way mammals can stay active even in cold conditions. Three, mammals feed their young on milk. The milk is made in specialized skin structures called mammary glands; hence our group's biological name, Mammalia. This book sets out to explore the world of the mammals - what they look like, their body structure, evolution, breeding habits, and behavior - and in doing so will hopefully cast some light on our place in this group.

MAMMALS AS ANIMALS
There are about 4,000 species (types) of mammals. Because of the number of domestic species, and the popularity of mammals in zoos, we are more familiar with them than other animal groups. Yet there are some 9,000 species of birds, 20,000 species of fish, and 100,000 species of spiders and scorpions. All these pale against the greatest animal group - the insects, with at least one million species, and possibly 10 times that number.

Noah's Ark took on board two of every mammal species - one male and one female

Making sense of mammals

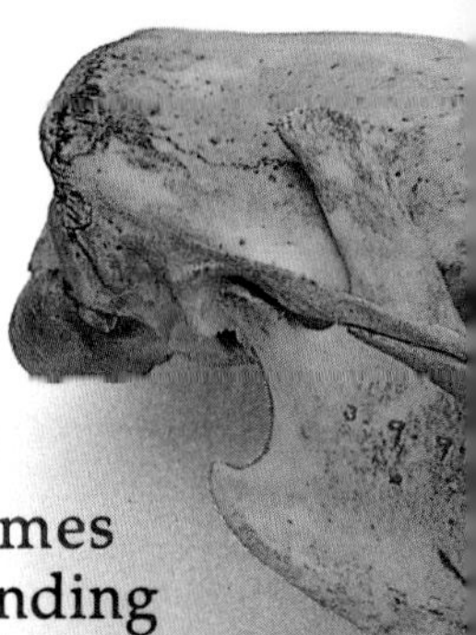

We can appreciate the beauty and wonder of mammals without knowing their scientific names or evolutionary origins. But a deeper understanding of body structure, behavior, and evolution needs, like any aspect of science, a framework for study. This framework is provided by taxonomy, the grouping and classifying of living things according to natural relationships. Every living animal has a scientific name that is recognized across the world and in all languages. This avoids confusion, since local or common names vary from country to country, and even from place to place within the same country. Each kind of animal is known as a species. Species are grouped together into genera, genera are grouped into families, families into orders, and orders into classes . . . and this is where we can stop, since all mammals belong to one class, Mammalia. The following four pages show the skulls of representatives of the 20 or so main orders of living mammals, and list the types of animals that belong in each one. The colored lines indicate their probable evolutionary relationships to one another.

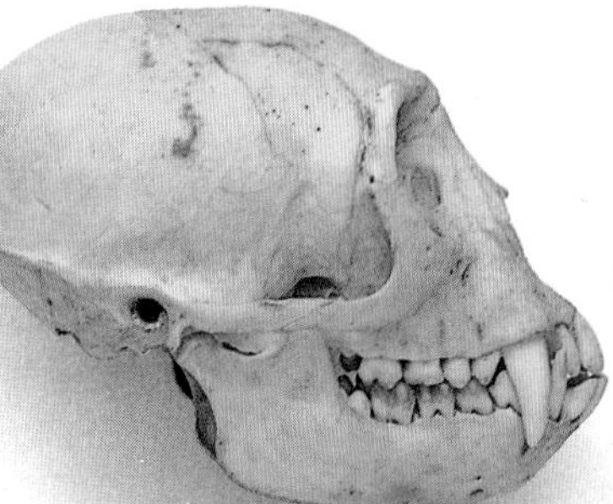

EDENTATES (Edentata)
Includes anteaters, armadillos, sloths.
About 30 species
Skull shown: Greater long-nosed armadillo
See also pp. 22, 27, 29, 51

Armadillo

Monkey

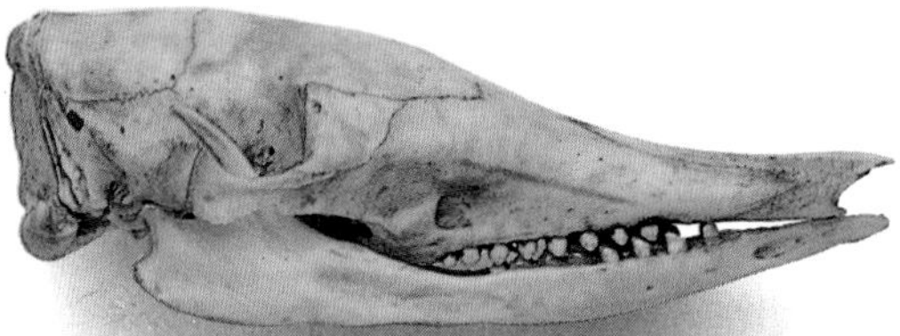

MONKEYS AND APES (Primates)
Includes lemurs, bushbabies, lorises, pottos, tarsiers, marmosets, tamarins, monkeys, apes, humans.
About 180 species
Skull shown: Vervet monkey
See also pp. 2, 3, 6-7, 16-17, 21, 22-3, 29, 37, 38, 44, 49, 58

MARSUPIALS OR POUCHED MAMMALS (Marsupialia)
Includes kangaroos, wallabies, wombats, opossums, dunnarts, bandicoots, cuscuses.
About 270 species
Skull shown: Mountain cuscus
See also pp, 3, 4, 10 20, 22, 27, 30-31

Kangaroo

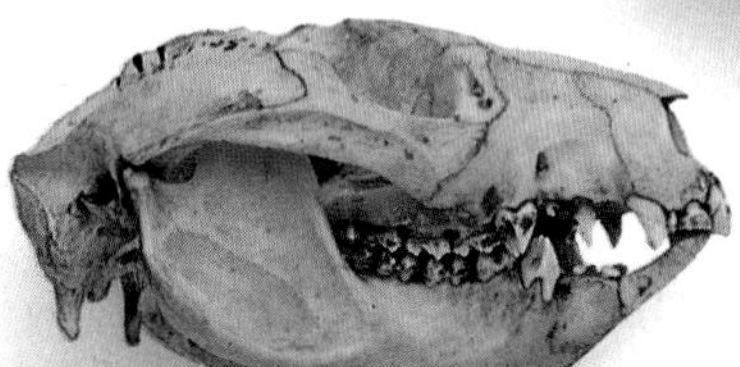

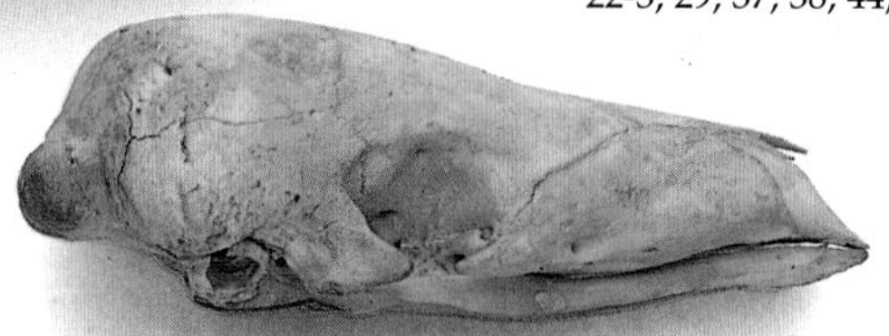

Pangolin

PANGOLINS (Pholidota)
Pangolins
About 7 species
Skull shown: Chinese pangolin
See also p. 27

Platypus

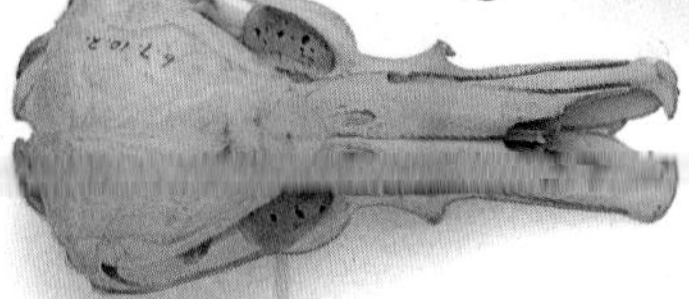

EGG-LAYING MAMMALS (Monotremata)
Platypuses, echidnas. Generally regarded as the most "primitive" mammals, since they lay eggs (like reptiles) and do not give birth to formed young.
3 species
Skull shown: Platypus
See also pp. 16, 25, 27, 30, 56

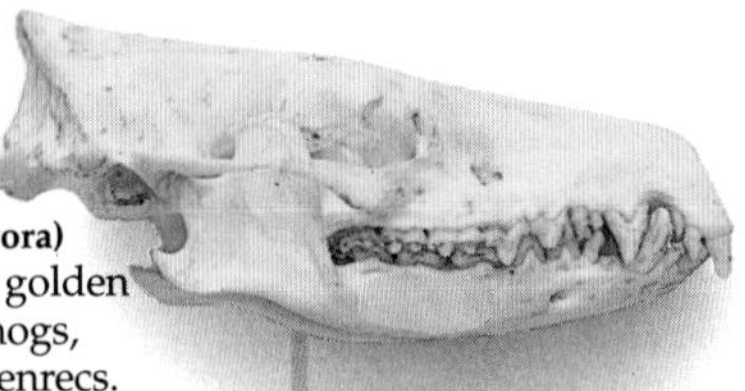

INSECTIVORES (Insectivora)
Includes shrews, moles, golden moles, desmans, hedgehogs, moonrats, solenodons, tenrecs.
About 375 species
Skull shown: Greater moonrat
See also pp. 3, 24-5, 51, 57, 61

Shrew

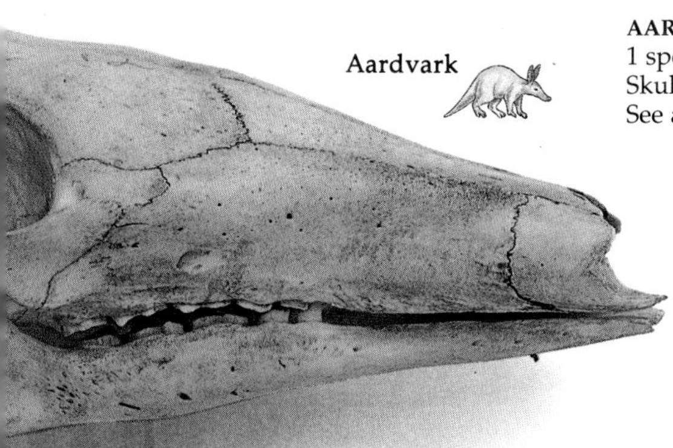

Aardvark

AARDVARK (Tubulidentata)
1 species
Skull shown: Aardvark
See also p. 51

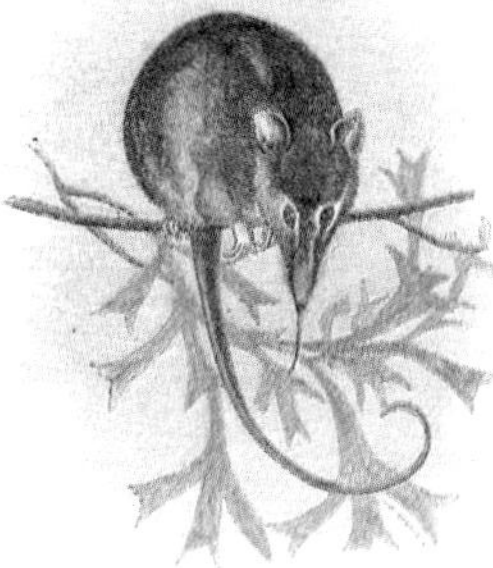

Honey possum

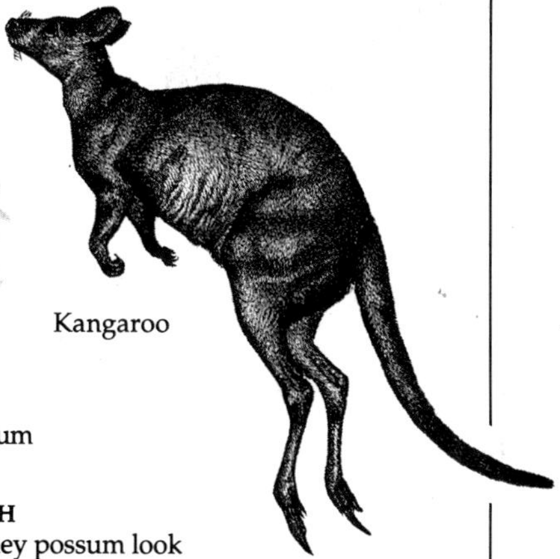

Kangaroo

BOUND BY THE POUCH
The kangaroo and honey possum look quite different, yet they are both marsupials. The important common feature is the pouch in which the baby suckles and grows after birth. Only marsupials have this feature.

Lion

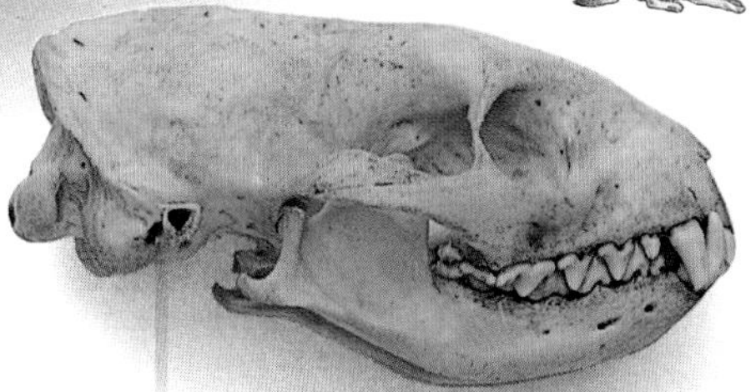

CARNIVORES (Carnivora)
Includes big and small cats, dogs, foxes, wolves, hyenas, bears, pandas, raccoons, weasels, stoats, badgers, skunks, otters, mongooses, civets.
About 230 species
Skull shown: Egyptian mongoose
See also pp. 2, 3, 4, 16-17, 21, 28-9, 34-9, 42-3, 46-7, 49, 50, 53, 56, 59, 60, 63

SEALS (Pinnipedia)
Seals, sea lions, walruses.
About 33 species
Skull shown: Gray seal
See also pp. 10, 20, 51, 59, 63

Seal

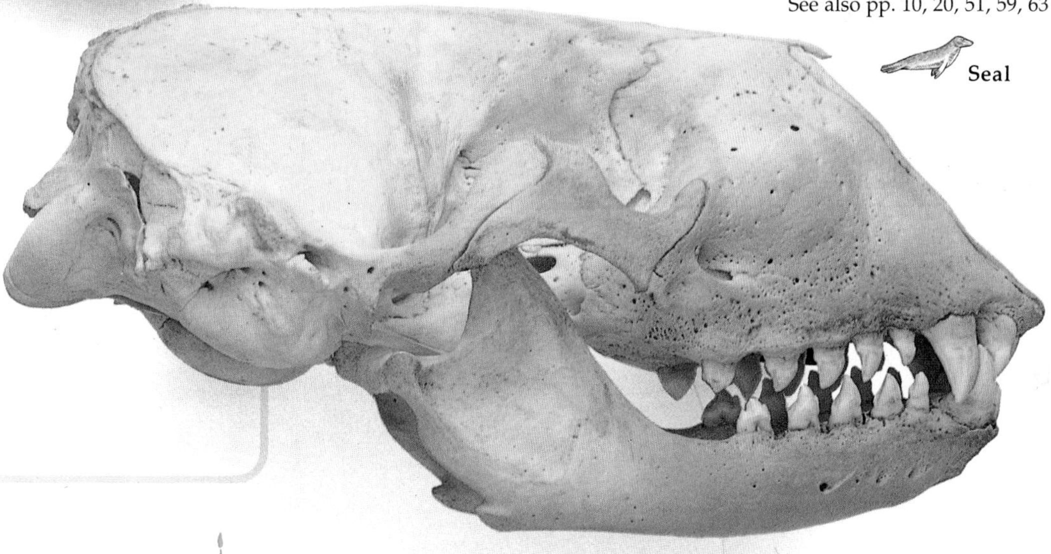

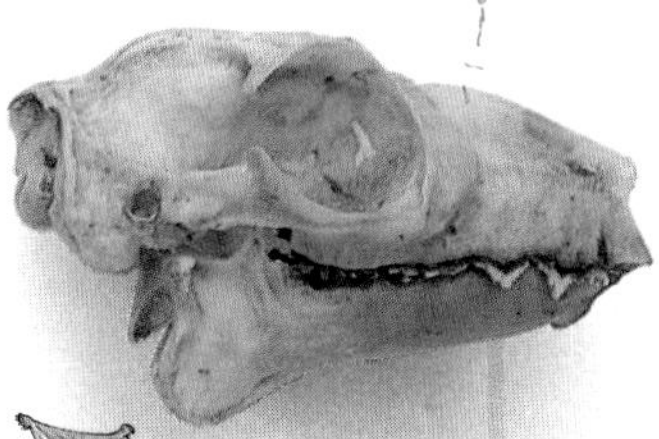

Colugo

COLUGOS (Dermoptera)
Also called flying lemurs.
2 species
Skull shown: Malayan colugo
See also p. 19

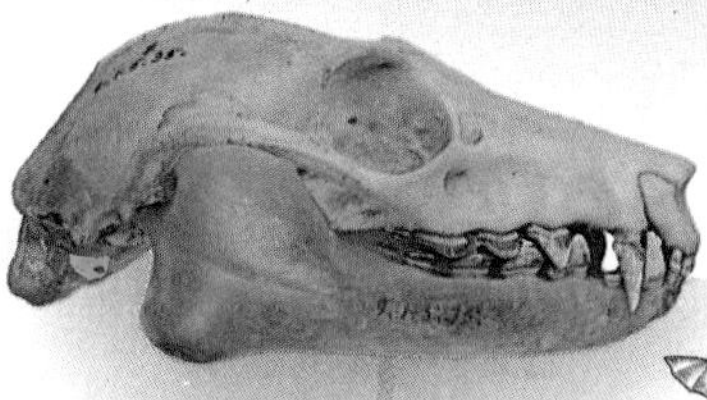

BATS (Chiroptera)
Includes flying foxes (fruit bats), vampires, and all other bats.
About 1,000 species (nearly one-quarter of all mammal species)
Skulls shown: Common flying fox
See also pp. 2, 18-19, 63

Bat

Rat
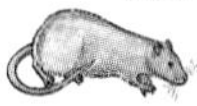

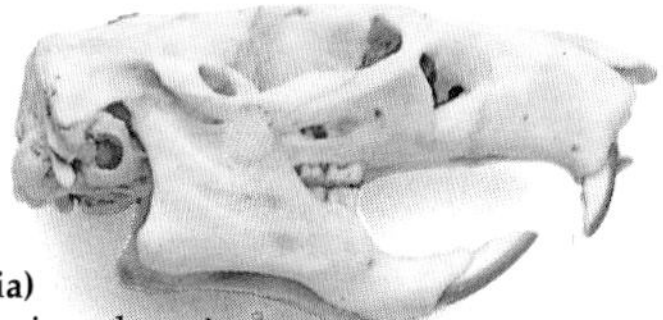

RODENTS (Rodentia)
Includes rats and mice, dormice, gerbils, beavers, squirrels, porcupines, chinchillas, pacas, voles, hamsters, chipmunks.
About 1,700 species
Skull shown: Giant pouched rat
See also pp. 2, 4, 5, 16, 20, 22-3, 27, 32-3, 44-5, 48-9, 51, 52-3, 54-5, 61, 63

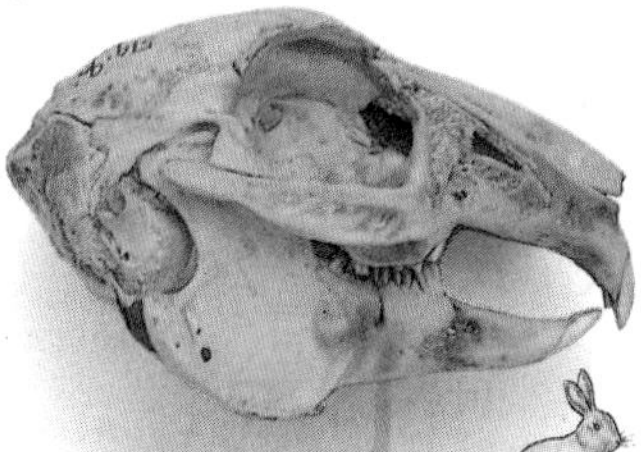

Rabbit

RABBITS AND HARES (Lagomorpha)
Includes rabbits, cottontails, jackrabbits, hares, pikas.
About 80 species
Skull shown: European rabbit
See also pp. 2, 4, 60

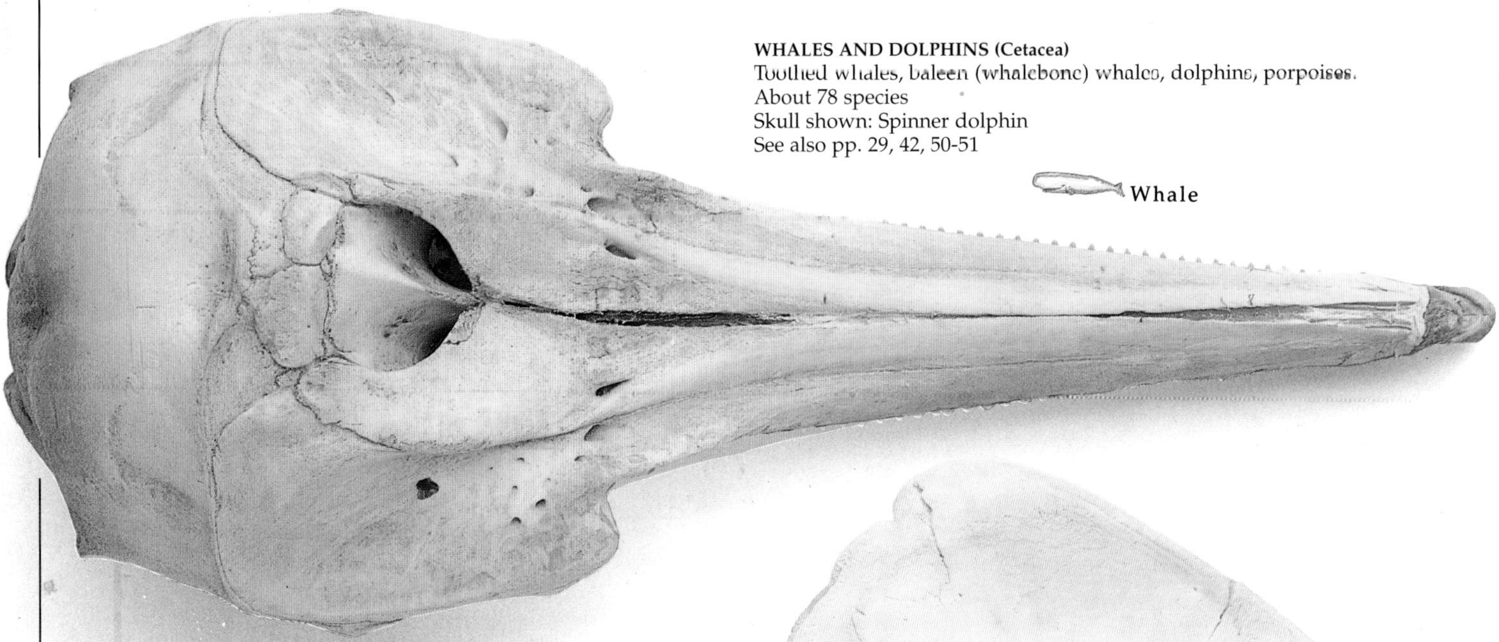

WHALES AND DOLPHINS (Cetacea)
Toothed whales, baleen (whalebone) whales, dolphins, porpoises.
About 78 species
Skull shown: Spinner dolphin
See also pp. 29, 42, 50-51

Whale

ODD-TOED HOOFED MAMMALS (Perissodactyla)
Horses, asses, zebras, rhinos, tapirs.
17 species
Skull shown: Brazilian tapir
See also pp. 23, 27, 28, 36, 44, 46, 50, 58

Tapir

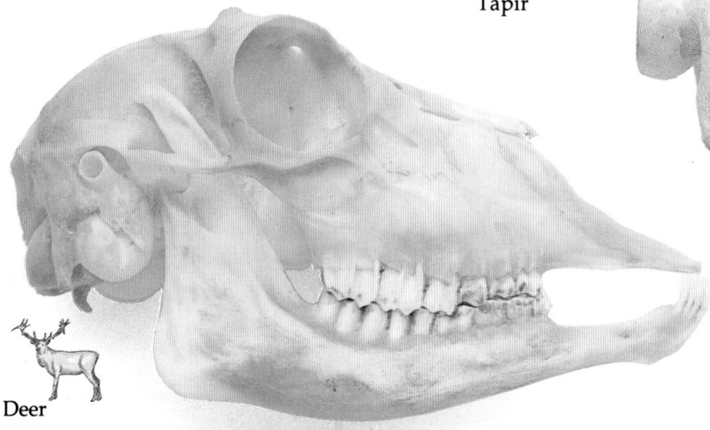

Deer

EVEN-TOED HOOFED MAMMALS (Artiodactyla)
Includes hippos, pigs, peccaries, camels, llamas, giraffes, deer, chevrotains, gazelles, antelopes, cattle, sheep, goats.
About 220 species
Skull shown: Goitered gazelle
See also pp. 3, 16, 20-21, 27, 28, 35, 48, 58, 63

Hyrax

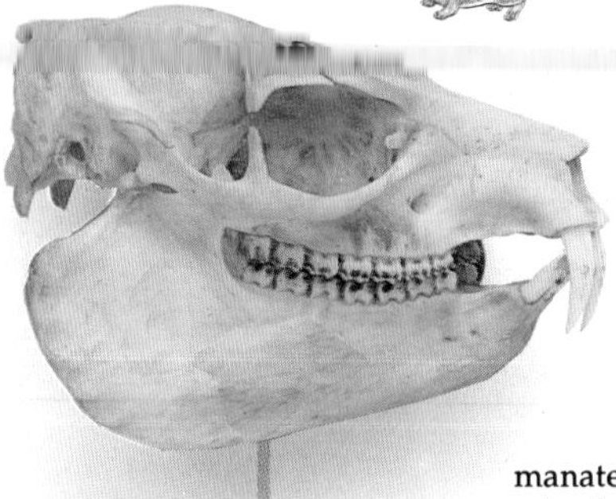

HYRAXES (Hyracoidea)
Bush hyraxes, tree hyraxes, rock hyraxes, dassies.
7 species
Skull shown: Southern tree hyrax
See also pp. 58

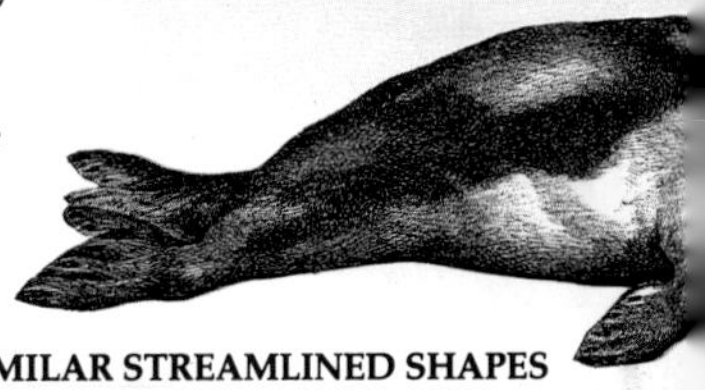

SIMILAR STREAMLINED SHAPES
Body shapes can be misleading. A seal and a manatee look similar - because they both live in water and have evolved a streamlined shape for swimming (convergent evolution). But their teeth, digestive systems, and other internal structures show that they are quite different and therefore placed in different orders.

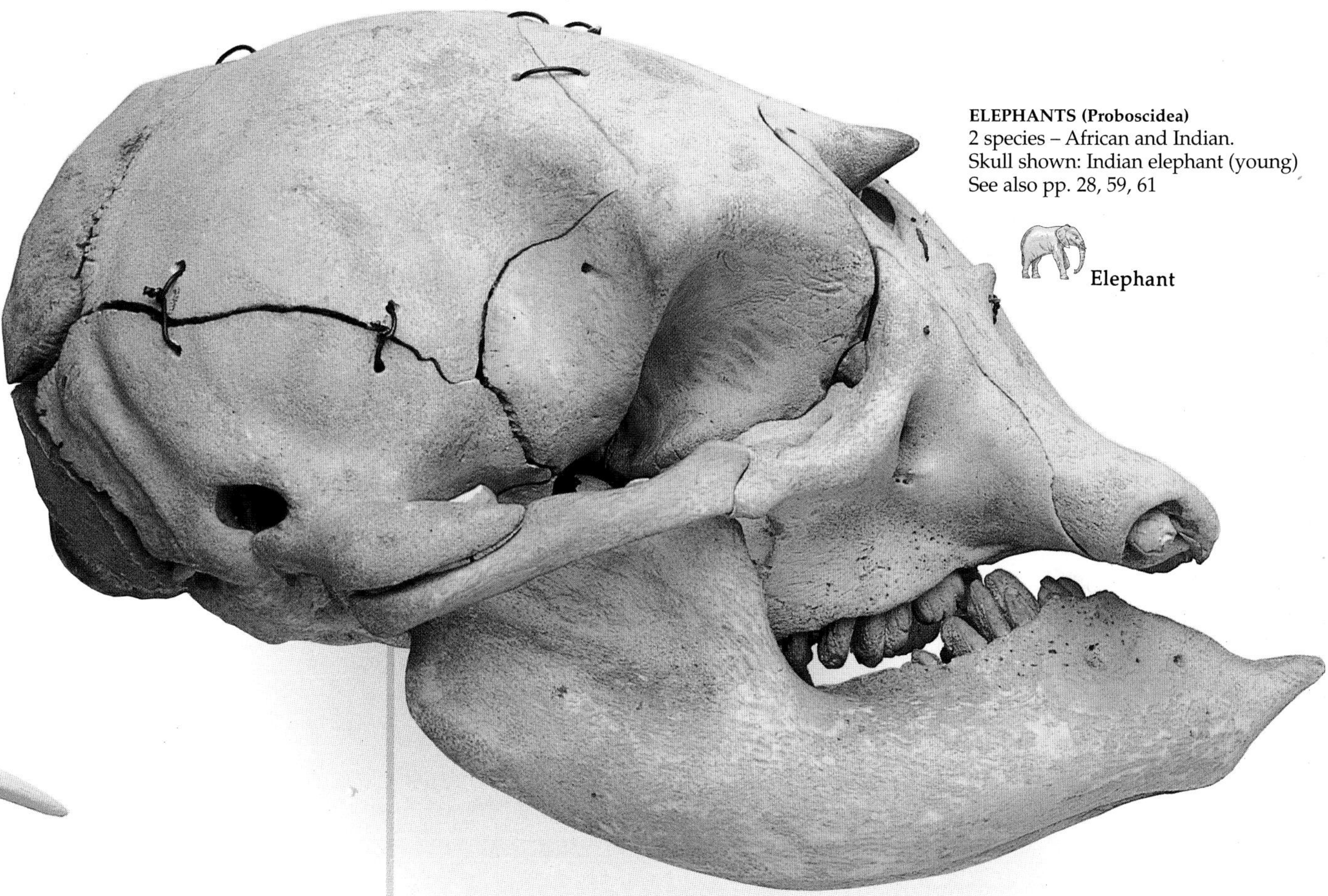

ELEPHANTS (Proboscidea)
2 species – African and Indian.
Skull shown: Indian elephant (young)
See also pp. 28, 59, 61

Elephant

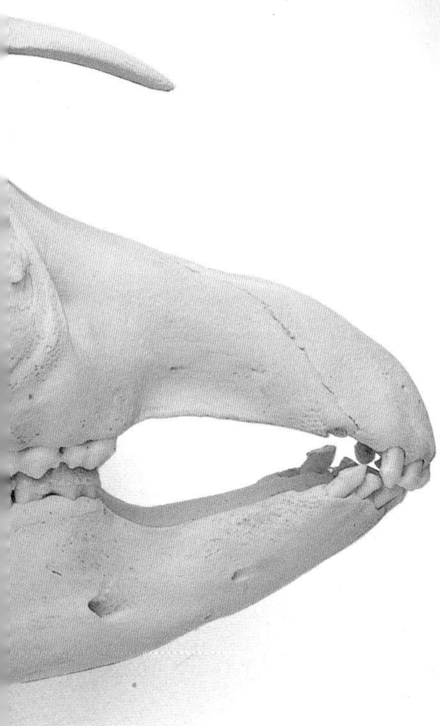

Order not shown is Scandentia (18 species) - tree shrews, tupais, and dendrogales or tree squirrels; elephant shrews (family Macroscelididae, 15 species) are classed under order Insectivora.

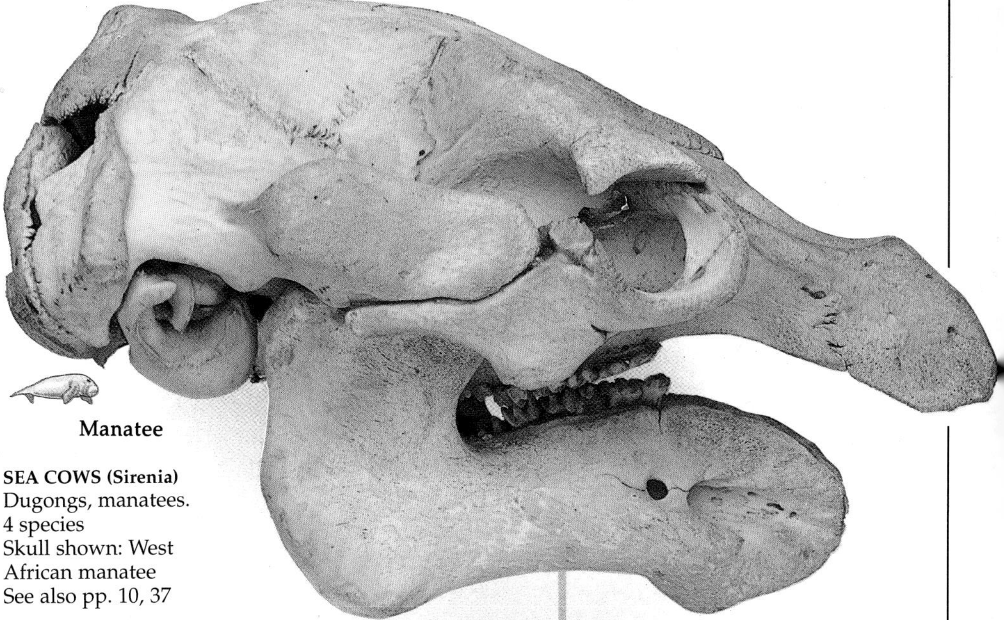

Manatee

SEA COWS (Sirenia)
Dugongs, manatees.
4 species
Skull shown: West African manatee
See also pp. 10, 37

Manatee

The evolution of mammals

An early rhino?

As far as we know, mammals appeared on Earth some 200 million years ago. We know because we have found their fossils: bones, teeth, and other parts that have been turned to stone and preserved in rocks. Since some of the features we recognize in living mammals (warm blood, fur, and milk) do not fossilize we must look for other clues. These must be based on the bones. So another two important features of being a mammal, alive or fossilized, are a particular kind of jaw (only one bone in the lower jaw, not several like the reptiles), and tiny bones in the middle ear cavity. Mammals did not exactly burst upon the evolutionary scene. During their first 100 million or so years, life on land was mainly dominated by huge dinosaurs, while pterosaurs flew above and ichthyosaurs swam in the sea. The first true mammals were probably small, shrewlike creatures that were active at night and fed by eating insects and stealing dinosaur eggs. As the dinosaurs died out, and finally disappeared some 65 million years ago, mammals filled their place.

Skull from above

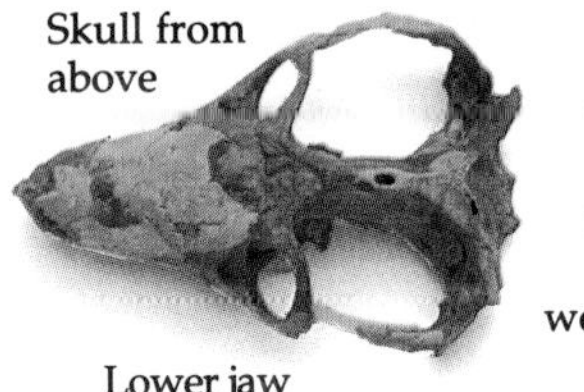

Lower jaw

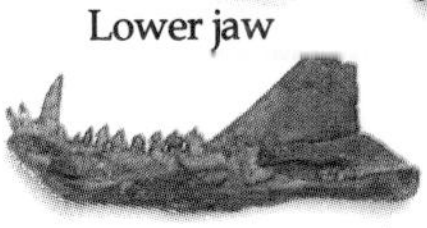

MAMMAL ANCESTOR?
The cynodonts were mammal-like reptiles of the Triassic period. Their teeth were not all the same, as in other reptile groups, but were different shapes, specialized to do certain jobs. This is one of the mammal's characteristics, although some modern species (such as the dolphins) have re-evolved teeth that are all the same, in response to their diet (p. 51). Species shown: *Thrinaxon liorhinus* (S. Africa)

ONE OF THE FIRST
Embedded in rocks laid down in the middle Jurassic, in what is now England, is this jaw of a triconodont. These creatures were some of the earliest mammals, and they were rat- to cat-size predators. Species shown: *Phascolotherium bucklandi* (Oxfordshire, England)

Lower jaw embedded in rock

Upper jaw

Lower jaw

SUCCESSFUL LINE
Freed from the domination of the dinosaurs, mammals changed rapidly during the Paleocene and Eocene as evolution "experimented" with new forms. Some died out. This one did, but its general design was continued to the present day. It was an early relative of the horse, from the Eocene epoch Species shown: *Hyracotherium vulpiceps* (Essex, England)

THE STAGE IS SET
Into this sort of world, populated by giant fern-like plants, fish, insects, and reptiles, the first mammals emerged some 200 million years ago.

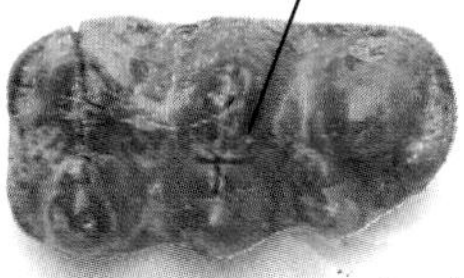

Mastodon tooth

TOUGH TOOTH
This tooth, 30 million years old, belonged to *Phiomia*, a mastodon that was a member of the order Proboscidea (p. 11). In life the creature was about 4 ft (1.2 m) long and looked like a pig-rhino cross. The term *mastodon*, meaning "breast-tooth," refers to the gradually evolving pattern on the chewing surface of these molar teeth.
Species shown: *Phiomia serridens* (Egypt)

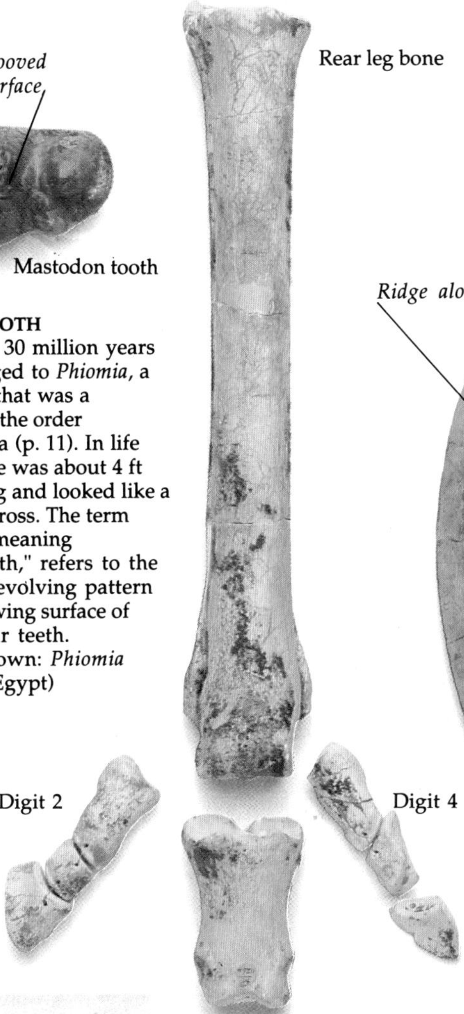

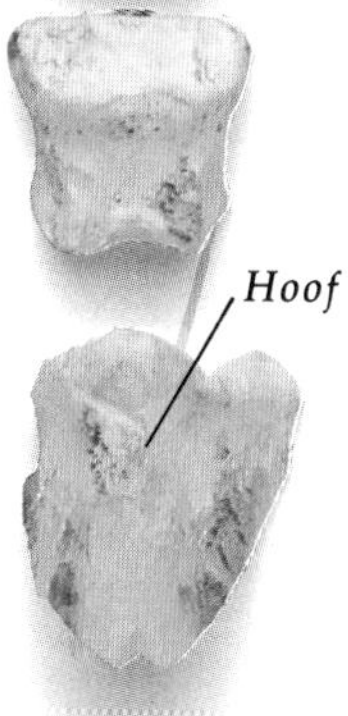

Borhyaena skull shown from side

FOSSIL MARSUPIAL MEAT EATER
In prehistoric times, marsupial mammals (p. 30) were more widespread than today. They evolved into forms that compare easily with most modern mammals. This one, *Borhyaena*, was a great hunter and must have competed for a meal with the great flightless birds of the Miocene.
Species shown: *Borhyaena tuberata* (Argentina)

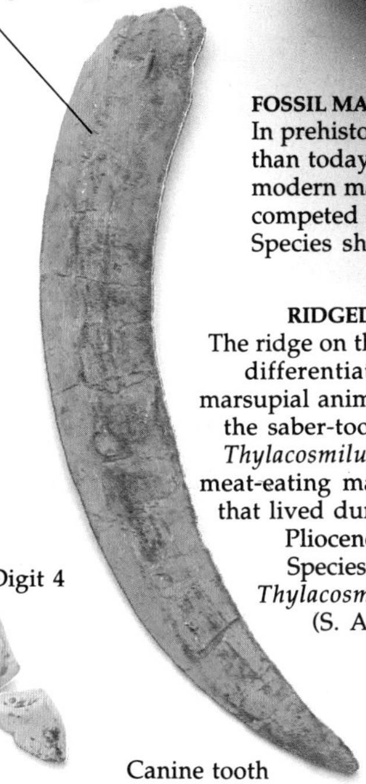

Canine tooth

RIDGED SABER
The ridge on the tooth differentiates this marsupial animal from the saber-tooth cats. *Thylacosmilus* was a meat-eating marsupial that lived during the Pliocene epoch.
Species shown: *Thylacosmilus* sp. (S. America)

MARSUPIAL GRINDERS
From looking at the teeth in the jaw we can see that *Protemnodon* was a marsupial herbivore (plant eater). It lived during the Pleistocene epoch.
Species shown: *Protemnodon antaeus* (Australia)

Lower jaw

MAMMOTH MOLAR
This enormous fossilized molar tooth shows the development of the grinding surface in the Proboscidea (compare it with the *Phiomia* tooth).
Species shown: *Mammuthus primigenius* (Essex, England)

Hipparion's probable appearance in life, about small-pony size

THREE-TOED HORSE
As the horses continued to evolve (see left), the toes gradually disappeared. This specimen is from the Miocene and shows a stage between the original mammalian five-toed foot and the one-toed foot of the modern horse (p. 58). Already the side toes are short and only the central (3rd) rests on the ground. This is not necessarily the ancestor of the modern horse, but evidence of its evolution.
Species shown: *Hipparion* sp. (Greece)

Molar tooth from side

TIME CHART SHOWING EVOLUTION OF MAMMALS (Millions of years ago)

PALEOZOIC ERA (Primary)						MESOZOIC ERA (Secondary)		
570	500	435	395	345	280	230	195	140
Cambrian period Trilobites become abundant.	**Ordovician period** Corals, brachiopods, nautiloids, and graptolites are common.	**Silurian period** Fish with jaws appear. Sea scorpions present.	**Devonian period** Fish become abundant. The first amphibians appear.	**Carboniferous period** The first reptiles and first winged insects appear. Amphibians become abundant.	**Permian period** Insects become diverse. Reptiles begin to take over the land.	**Triassic period** The first mammals appear. Reptiles are abundant.	**Jurassic period** The first birds appear. The heyday of dinosaurs.	**Cretaceous period** Mammals and birds begin to diversify. Dinosaurs become less common and finally die out.

The mammals diversify

Giant sloth, more than 12 ft (4 m) tall (Pleistocene)

THE MAMMALS CONTINUED to evolve and diversify (change) and during the Miocene and Pliocene epochs they became more modern looking. In Asia, North America, and Europe, more than three quarters of Pliocene mammal species belonged to groups in existence today. In Australia and South America, land masses isolated for millions of years by continental drift, there were numerous marsupial (p. 30) mammals. Two million years ago South America became joined to North America, and more placental (p. 34) mammals from the north spread south. Australia is still physically isolated, and still has a wider range of marsupials than South America.

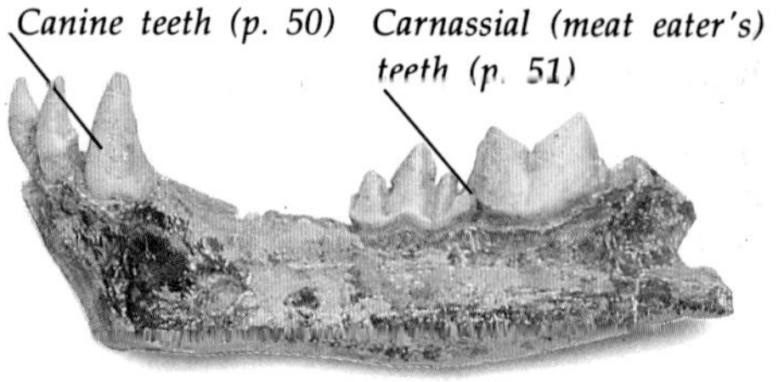

Lower jaw of *Machairodus*

CONSPICUOUS CANINES
This lower jaw is from a Miocene saber-toothed cat (the "saber tooth" was in the upper jaw). Well-developed muscle-anchorage points in the face and neck region indicate it opened its mouth wide and stabbed its prey to death.
Species shown: *Machairodus aphanistus* (Greece)

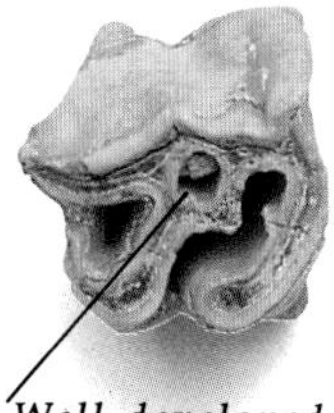

ICE AGE RHINO
An upper molar tooth from a woolly rhino of the Pleistocene shows how the folds of enamel and dentine (p. 50) were ground flat by chewing.
Species shown: *Coelodonta antiquitatis* (Devon, England)

Upper jaw of *Dorudon*

WHALE'S BONE
In the water, as on the land, new mammal species were evolving while others died out. This is the upper jaw of an extinct Eocene whale showing serrated (notched) teeth for gripping slippery prey.
Species shown: *Dorudon osiris* (Egypt)

ANCIENT GIRAFFE *below*
Sivatherium was a Pleistocene relative of the giraffe, although with shorter legs and neck and longer horns than today's version.
Species shown: *Sivatherium maurusium* (Tanzania)

Reconstruction of *Sivatherium*, showing antlers behind bony forehead "cones"

A KNUCKLE WALKER?
This is the "toenail" bone from *Chalicotherium*, an extinct Miocene mammal related to rhinos and horses. Its front limbs were much longer than its back ones, and it may have knuckle-walked like a gorilla.
Species shown: *Chalicotherium rusingense* (Kenya)

Plesiaddax skull from the side

UNGULATE SKULL
Many new kinds of ungulates (hoofed mammals) came during the Miocene, especially horned ones. *Plesiaddax* was a type of antelope related to the musk ox of today.
Species shown: Plesiaddax depereti (China)

Antler of *Sivatherium*

CENOZOIC ERA (Tertiary period)					Quaternary	
66	55	37.5	24	5	1.7	0.01
Palaeocene epoch Mammals rapidly diversify, but are still unlike those alive today.	**Eocene epoch** The first primates and bats appear. Early horses appear.	**Oligocene epoch** The first mastodons appear, and many relatives of the rhino.	**Miocene epoch** Apes present. More modern plant-feeding mammals become abundant.	**Pliocene epoch** The first humans evolve.	**Pleistocene epoch** Ice Age mammals abundant as the ice caps advance and retreat.	**Holocene epoch** Modern mammals. Humans increase on all continents.

RECENTLY EXTINCT CAVE DWELLER
The cave bear was larger than any bear of today, and it was around with the early humans, as the scene below depicts. Some of its remains come from caves, especially in the Pyrenees and Alps of Europe.
Species shown:
Ursus spelaeus (Germany)

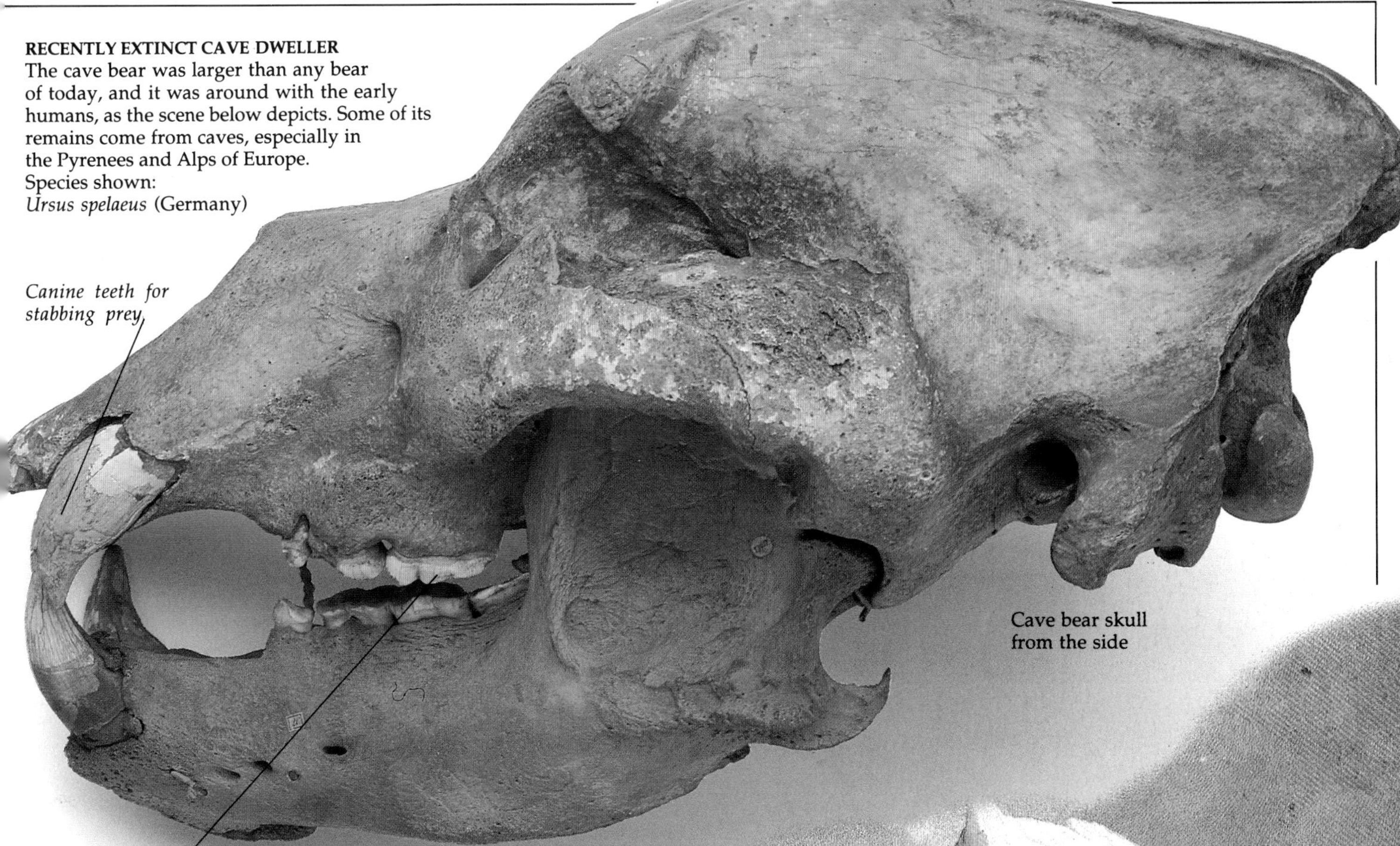

Cave bear skull from the side

CAVE TAKEOVER
This rather fanciful Pleistocene scene nevertheless shows some of the mammals with which our ancestors shared the countryside.

Mammal senses

THE CAT'S WHISKERS
Or in this case, the mouse's whiskers! Whiskers are longer-than-normal hairs with sensory cells embedded in the skin to detect any movement. Most whiskers are on the face, but some mammals have them on their legs, feet, or back.

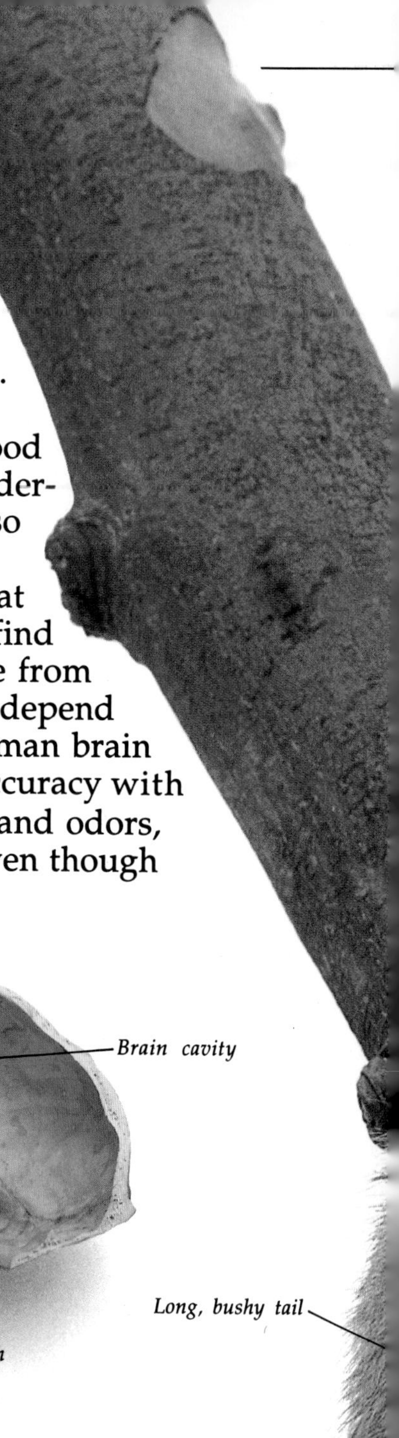

ONE REASON for the mammals' success is their "good sense" - their generally well-developed senses of sight, hearing, smell, taste, and touch. Each sense has been molded by evolution to fit its owner's way of life. Good vision would be of little use to an underground mammal like a mole (p. 56), so this creature has poor eyesight; but it has an extremely sensitive muzzle that combines touch and smell in order to find food (chiefly earthworms that emerge from the walls of its burrow). We humans depend on our sense of vision. It is estimated that four fifths of what the human brain knows comes in via the eyes. So it is difficult for us to imagine the accuracy with which a mammal with a good nose smells the world through scents and odors, or how a bat hears its surroundings by echoed squeaks (p. 19). Yet, even though we depend on our eyes so much, our vision is not tremendous - other mammals, such as some species of squirrels, have much sharper sight. On the plus side, however, the primates (including humans and bush babies) are the main mammalian group with color vision. Most mammals see the world in black and white.

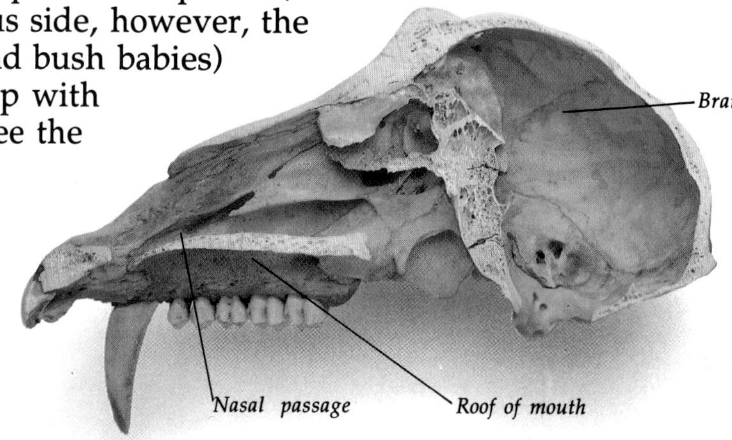

SKULLFUL OF SENSES
This cutaway view of a baboon's skull shows how a mammal's main senses are concentrated in the head. Bony cavities protect the brain, the eyes, the organs of smell, and the tasting tongue. The mammalian brain is large in proportion to the body, as it has to make sense of the mass of information sent from the rest of the body.

PRICKING UP THE EARS
Many mammals, including dogs, have a good sense of hearing and can move their ears in the direction of a sound. This gives greater accuracy in pinpointing where the sound is coming from.

HUNTING BY TOUCH
The platypus grubs about in rivers and streams for food, and finds its prey of water worms, insects, and crayfish almost entirely by touch, as its bill is extremely sensitive.

THE WORLD IN SMELLS
A pig with a trained nose snuffles for truffles - underground fungi that will be dug up by its owner and sold as an expensive delicacy.

FOOD-TESTING TONGUE
This lion tests its food partly by smell and partly by taste. But tongues not only taste, they do other jobs. A mammal licking its lips is cleaning its face (pp. 44-47).

FACING THE FRONT
The bush baby seems all eyes and ears. This shy, nocturnal (active at night) member of the order Primates (p. 8) has enormous eyes which can see in the darkest forest night in order to locate prey and leap from branch to branch to avoid predators. Bush babies are especially good at tracking small flying insects with their large swiveling ears; then, clinging with the back feet, they extend body and arms to snatch the insect as it flies past. The origin of this mammal's name may be from one of its calls, which is remarkably like the cry of a human baby - or it may be that the animal's appealing features look like those of a baby.

Senegal bush baby

EYES AT NIGHT
This odd-eyed white cat has one yellow eye and one blue eye. When photographed at night using a flash its yellow eye reflects green from a shiny layer (tapetum) in the back of the eye.The blue eye lacks a tapetum so the blood vessels at the back of the eye glow red.

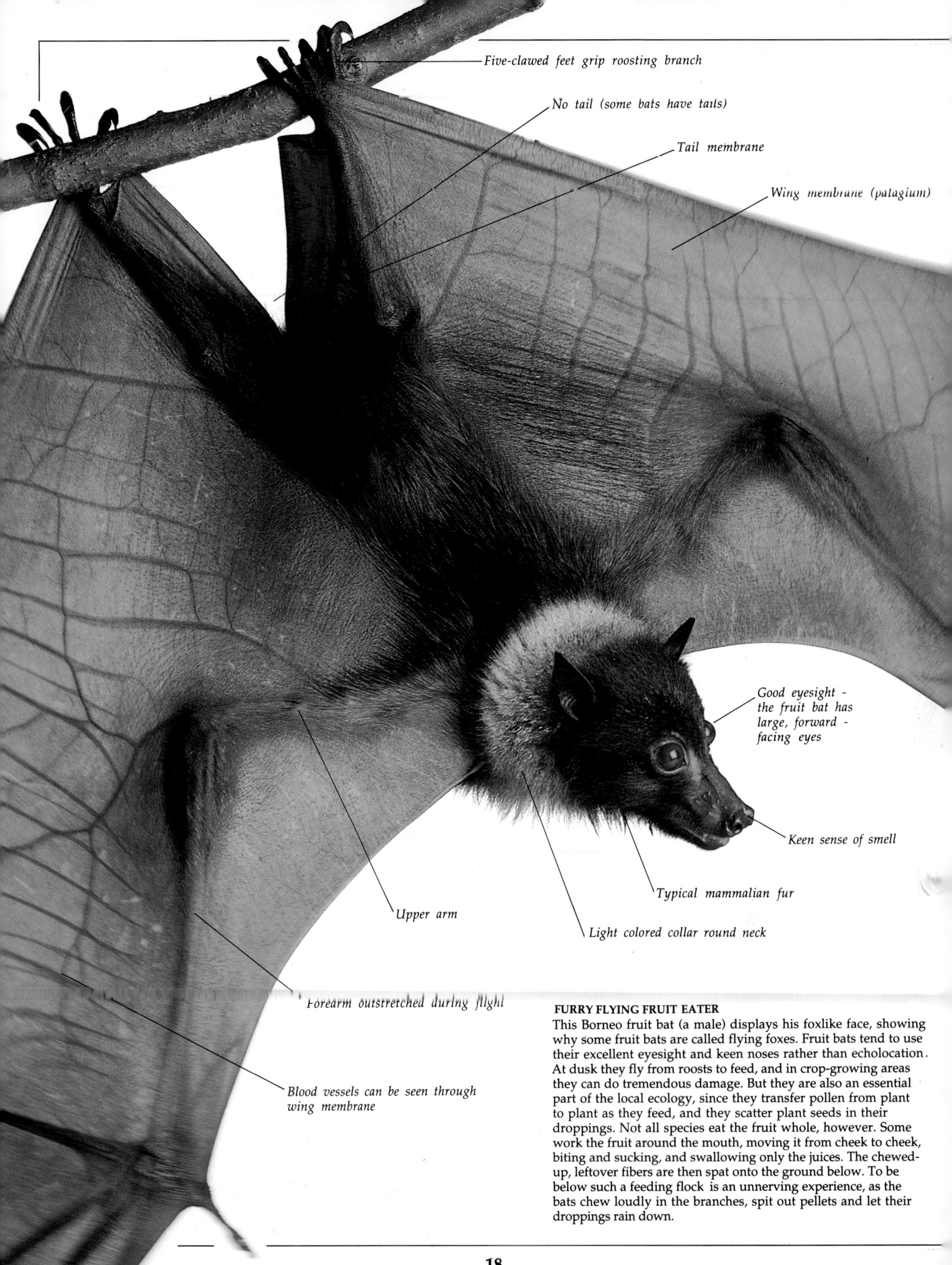

FURRY FLYING FRUIT EATER

This Borneo fruit bat (a male) displays his foxlike face, showing why some fruit bats are called flying foxes. Fruit bats tend to use their excellent eyesight and keen noses rather than echolocation. At dusk they fly from roosts to feed, and in crop-growing areas they can do tremendous damage. But they are also an essential part of the local ecology, since they transfer pollen from plant to plant as they feed, and they scatter plant seeds in their droppings. Not all species eat the fruit whole, however. Some work the fruit around the mouth, moving it from cheek to cheek, biting and sucking, and swallowing only the juices. The chewed-up, leftover fibers are then spat onto the ground below. To be below such a feeding flock is an unnerving experience, as the bats chew loudly in the branches, spit out pellets and let their droppings rain down.

Flying mammals

Pegasus - the legendary flying horse

MANY MAMMALS can leap and bound. Some can swim and dive. But only the bats can fly. Bats are the second most numerous group of mammals, in terms of species (p. 9). They vary enormously in size, from the tiny hog-nosed bat with a wingspan of 5 in (13 cm) to the large flying foxes with a body the size of a small dog and outstretched wings 6 ft (2 m) across.

The bat's flapping wings, unique among mammals, are made of thin sheets of muscle and elastic fibers covered by skin. The bones of the arm and second to fifth fingers support the wing; the "thumb" (first finger) is like a claw and used for crawling about, grooming, and, in some species, fighting and holding food. The muscles that power the wings are the ones you use to flap your arms, but proportionally many times stronger. Some bats can fly at more than 50 kph (30 mph). Bats are also among the most sociable of mammals. They roost together in their thousands in a cave or other suitable site. Some species cooperate in the nightly search for food. Males and females call to each other during the breeding season, and baby bats jammed like pink jelly into nursery roosts squeak loudly as the mothers return from hunting.

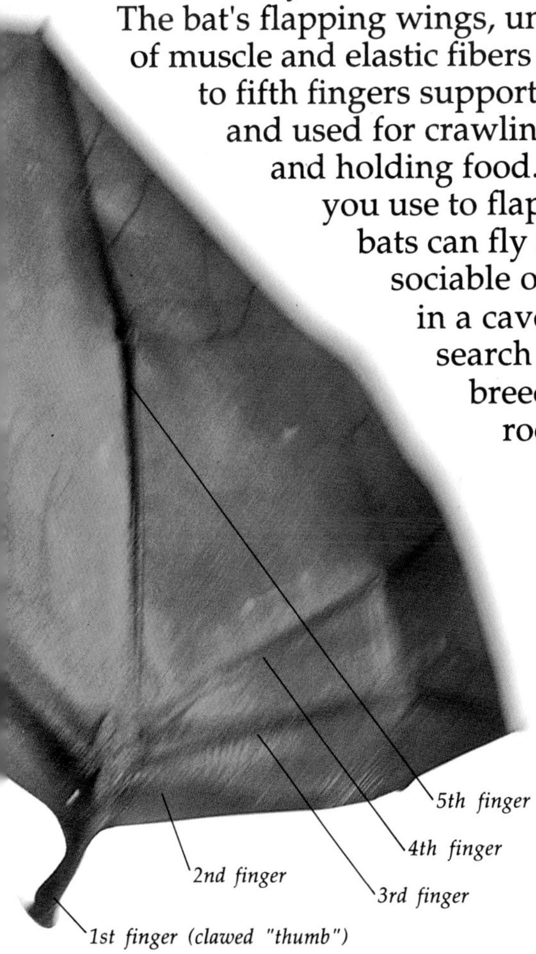

BAT BABIES *left*
Clinging on to their mother's furry abdomen, bat babies suckle milk, just like other mammals.

GLIDERS *right*
Bats are the only mammals capable of flight, but other mammals such as the marsupial gliders and colugos glide on the air using a membrane more like a parachute than a flapping wing.

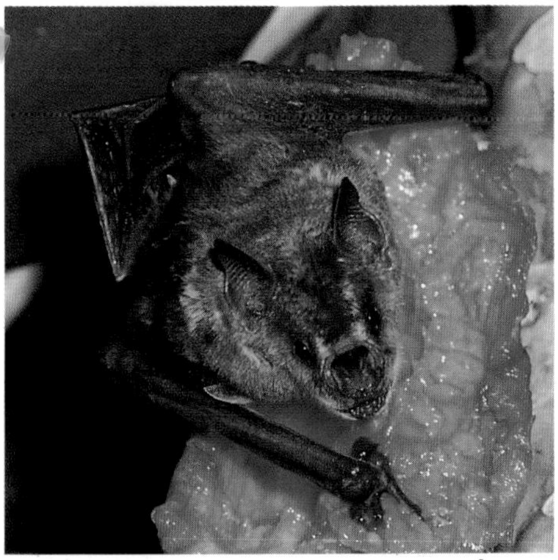

FROM MOTHS TO BUDS TO BLOOD
Most bats are insectivores, eating moths, midges, flies, and other nighttime flying creatures. The fruit bat (shown here) feeds on fruit, buds, and soft plant parts. The vampire bat feeds on blood.

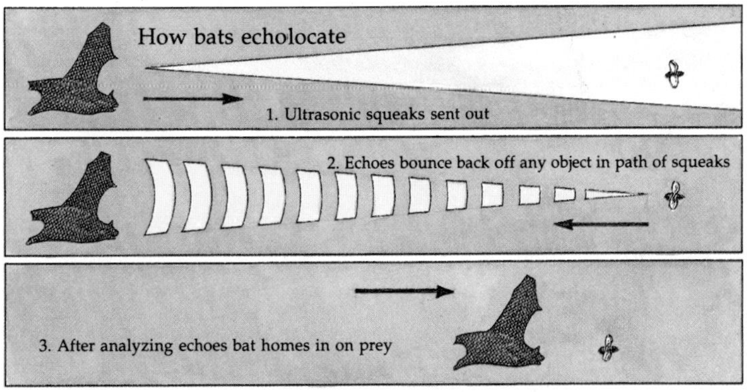

"SEEING" WITH SOUND
In fact bats hear in the dark, using echolocation. They send out high-pitched squeaks through the mouth (1). The sound waves bounce off anything in their path and return to the bat's ears as echoes (2). The bat's brain computes the pattern of echoes, forming a "sound picture." The bat then homes in on the moth (3).

A VARIETY OF FACES
Among mammals, bats have some of the most interesting faces.

Horse-shoe bat

Leaf-nosed bat

Bat with fringed tongue

Furry coats

FUR, WHISKERS, WOOL, prickles, spines, and even certain horns - these are all made from hair, one of the mammal's trademarks. The advantages of a furry coat have helped the mammal group to success. Most important is the ability of hair to trap air and keep out cold and heat, wind and rain, and so insulate the mammal's body from the surroundings. Hairs grow from tiny pits in the skin, called follicles. They consist of cells cemented together and toughened with keratin, the same fibrous protein substance that strengthens the skin. Not all mammals have hair. Some, like the whales, lost it during evolution.

All the furs shown here come from museum collections - no animals were killed for this book.

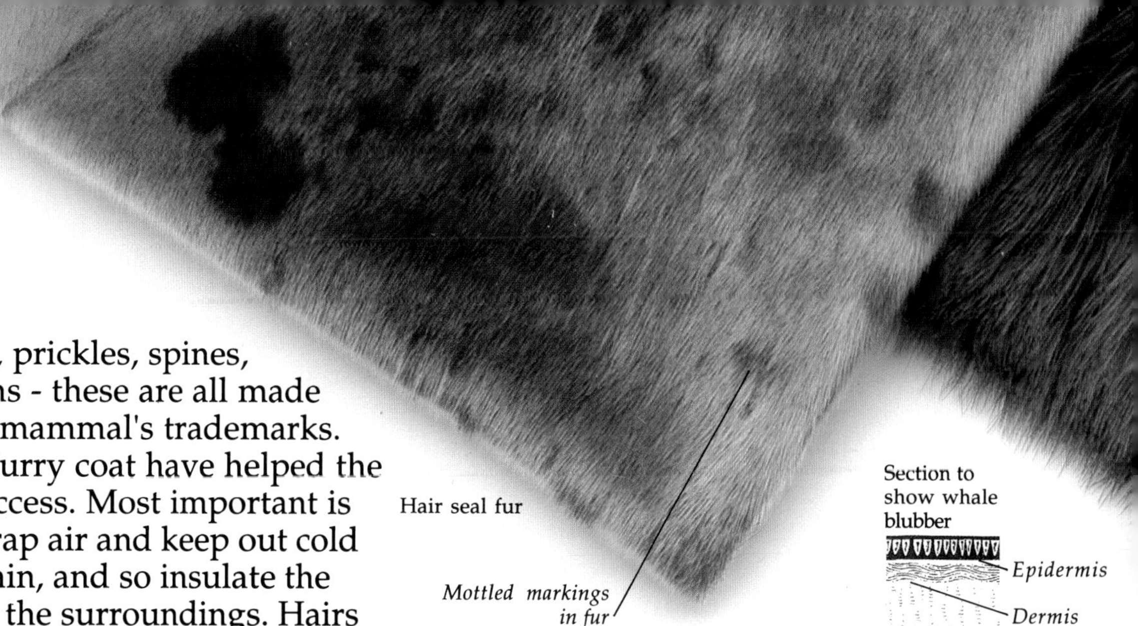

Hair seal fur

Mottled markings in fur

WATER TIGHT SEAL
The seal's skin contains many sebaceous (grease) glands that make its fur oily and water repellent. (Under the fur is a layer of blubber, like the whale's.) Native peoples such as the Inuit (below) hunt seals for meat and also for their skins, made into boots and garments.

KILLED FOR BLUBBER
Whales do not have fur to insulate them from the cold ocean water. This job is done by blubber, a layer of fatty tissue under the skin, which also streamlines the whale's shape for efficient swimming. In some whales the blubber is 20 in (50 cm) thick. Processed blubber, or whale oil, lit millions of lamps in days gone by and was also used for making lubricants, soap, cosmetics, margarine, and paint.

Section to show whale blubber

WOOL FOR WEARING
Sheep have been bred for their fur - wool - for centuries. Sheep's wool is a good insulator, absorbent yet springy, and takes up colored dyes well. More than half the world's wool comes from the Southern Hemisphere; three quarters of it is used in the Northern Hemisphere.

Spun and dyed wool, ready for weaving or knitting

Freshly sheared wool contains lanolin (wool grease) used in cosmetics

Inuit wearing seal fur hood

FURRY SNOW
The Arctic fox grows a beautiful all-white winter coat to camouflage it in its snowy landscape. Another color form, the blue, is grayish to brown in winter.

HAIRS ON GUARD
The opossum of North America has straight fur, unlike its marsupial cousin from Australia (right). The long, light guard hairs can clearly be seen projecting from the deep underfur.

POSSUM'S PELT
Australian possums tend to have crinkly or crimped hairs. The common brush-tailed possum is a cat-size, tree-dwelling species. One of its local names is "silver-gray," because of its fur.

Opossum fur

Possum fur

Polar color form Arctic fox fur

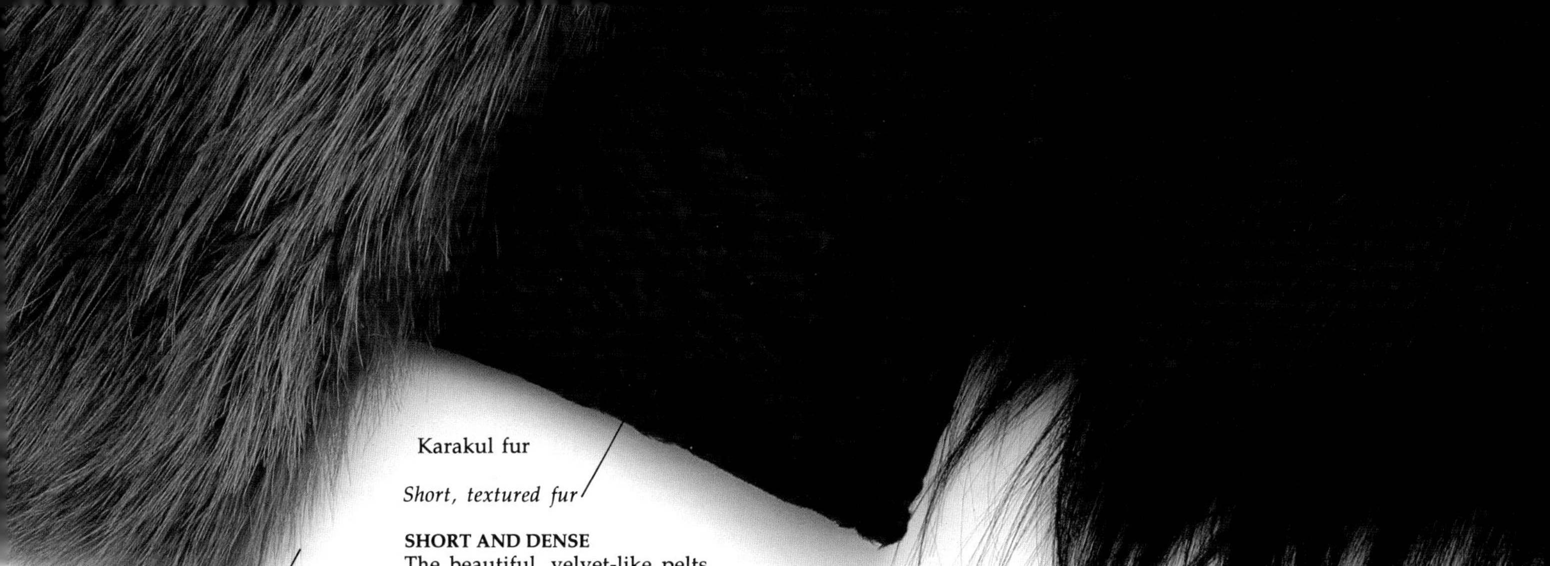

Karakul fur

Short, textured fur

SHORT AND DENSE
The beautiful, velvet-like pelts of young karakul sheep are known as "Persian lamb." Sheep were domesticated some 10-12,000 years ago, and today there are about 350 breeds, raised for meat as well as wool.

Beaver fur

Long guard hairs

KILLED FOR PELTS
Like many mammals', the beaver has two types of fur. One is a dense covering of short brown hairs - the underfur. The other is a sparser growth of longer, thicker hairs called the guard coat. The guard coat gives protection and camouflage; the underfur supplies insulation and waterproofing. Hunting North American beavers for their pelts (furred skins) was so profitable that wars were fought over land ownership, and the beaver fur trade helped open up much of North America in the 1700s and 1800s.

Colobus monkey fur

Long, thick hairs

LONG AND LUXURIANT
Some species of colobus monkey became rare because of being hunted for their fur, with its long, silky-looking hairs. The satanic black colobus has all-over, shiny black fur. Sadly, uninformed tourists still buy decorations and rugs made from colobus coats.

WATERPROOF FUR
Despite spending large amounts of its time under water, the water vole does not get "wet" as its long guard hairs keep the underfur dry.

NOT "NAKED"
We may think of ourselves as "naked apes," but we have lots of hairs. They are small and not very visible on the body, yet human head hair is typically mammalian. Fashions through the ages have sometimes emphasized hairiness, such as the wig (left) worn by this learned judge.

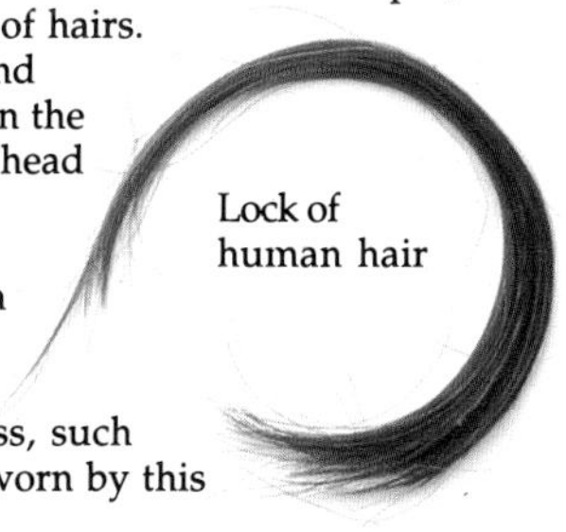

Lock of human hair

WARNING STRIPES
The skunk's distinctive stripes stand out as a warning sign. If a predator tries to molest the skunk it carries out its threat display, raising its tail and stamping. Should the molester ignore the warning, the skunk may turn and spray it with foul liquid from two anal glands.

BEAUTIFUL BELLY
Most spotted cats have spotted bellies. Lynx frequently have spotted backs as well.

Distinctive black and white stripes

Skunk fur

Lynx fur

Spotted belly fur

Hiding in the open

SMALL PLANT-EATING MAMMALS are very vulnerable when feeding out in the open. They have few ways of defending themselves from their many enemies. Camouflage- resembling and blending in with the surroundings - helps them to remain undetected as long as they stay still. Predators, too, employ camouflage in order to sneak up unseen on their prey. Fur is well suited to this purpose. Variations in length and color result in many different kinds of shading and patterning (p. 20).

BUILT-IN CAMOUFLAGE
Algae (tiny plants) grow on the coat of the slow-moving South American two-toed sloth. Its long outer guard hairs (p. 20) have grooves on them in which the algae grow. When the sloth is still (which it often is) in the dim forest light it merges with the foliage.

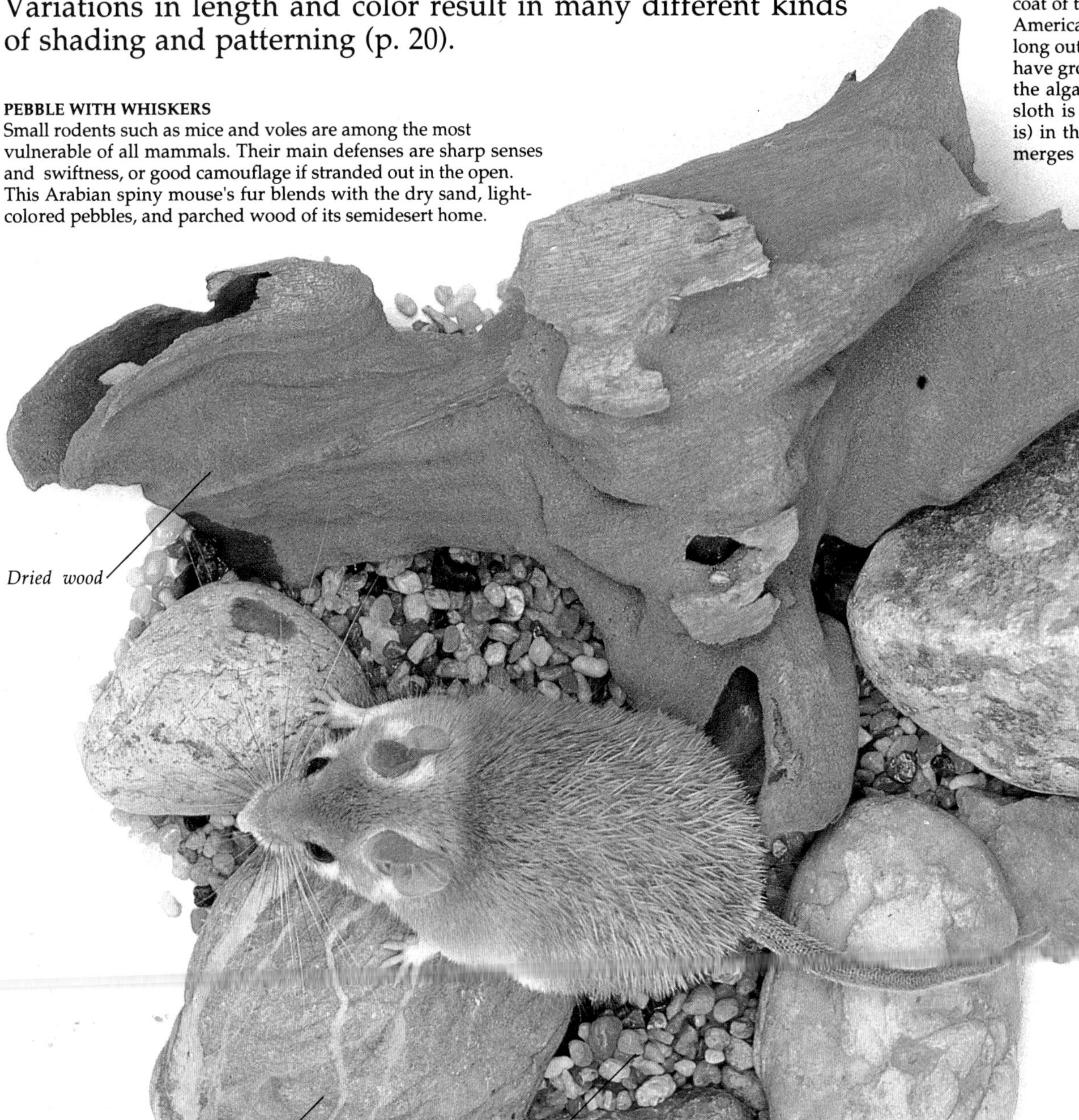

PEBBLE WITH WHISKERS
Small rodents such as mice and voles are among the most vulnerable of all mammals. Their main defenses are sharp senses and swiftness, or good camouflage if stranded out in the open. This Arabian spiny mouse's fur blends with the dry sand, light-colored pebbles, and parched wood of its semidesert home.

LEAF WITH A TAIL
Meadow voles live in a variety of places, from grassland to woods and streambanks. They forage on the ground, which is usually littered with dark, dead, or dying leaves and other plant parts. Voles are very busy animals, being active more or less around the clock, so visual camouflage is very important. A vole alerted by the soft wingbeat of a hunting bird might freeze in its tracks. In the dim light of dawn or dusk, or in the dappled shade under trees, it would be hard to spot from above - as shown by this owl's-eye view.

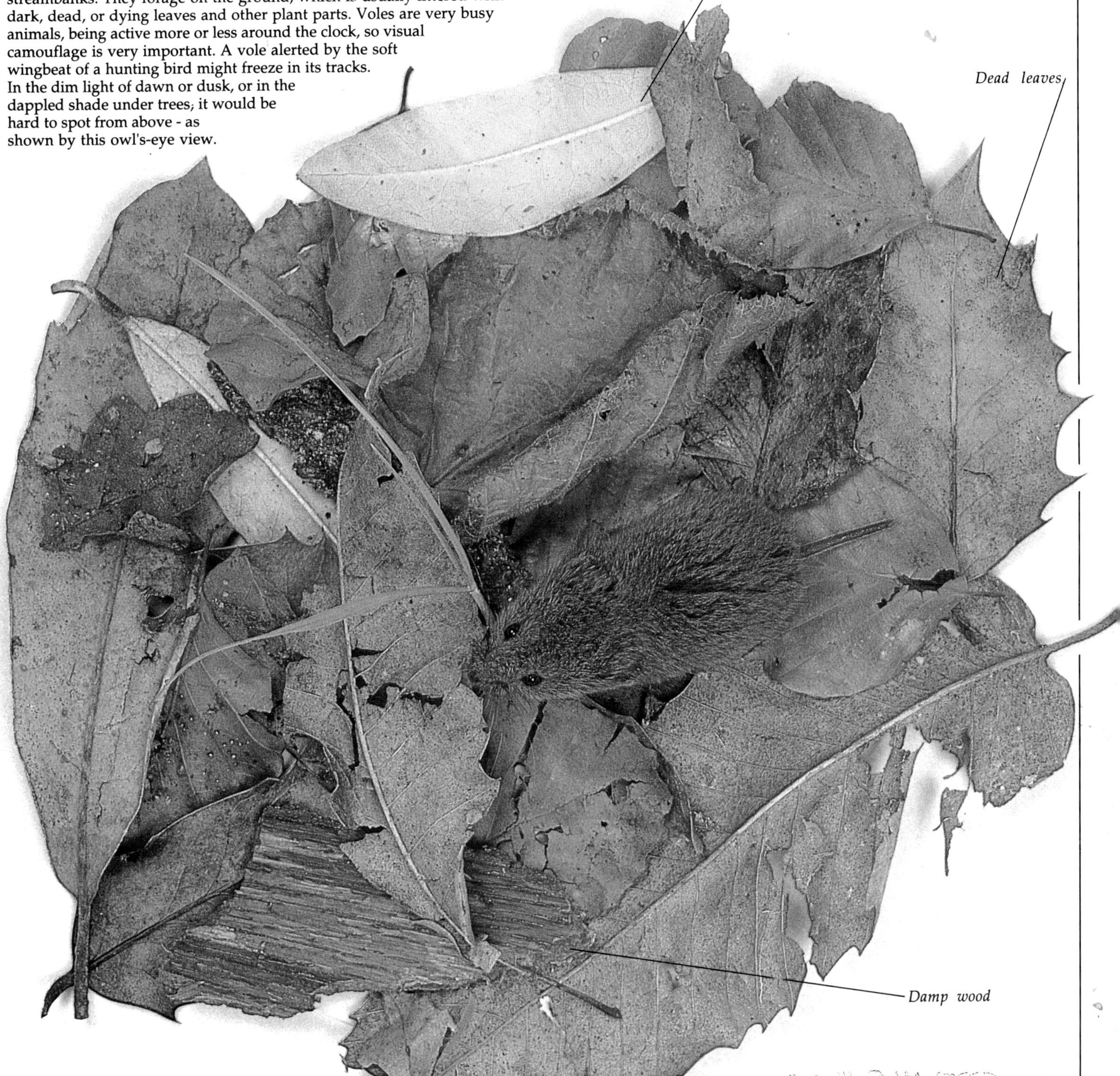

HIDING FROM THE ENEMY
Humans at war imitate nature and camouflage themselves, their vehicles, and their weapons. Standard combat clothes are "natural" greens and browns, mottled and patched to break up the soldier's outline in woods and scrubland. Snow-country outfits must be warm and white, like the Arctic fox's winter coat (p. 29).

DISGUISING THE OUTLINE
The Malayan tapir's striking coloration of white back and belly but black everything else is a fine example of "disruptive coloration." In the dark night-time forest the pattern breaks up the tapir's bulky body outline, making its distinctive shape less recognizable to predators. The young tapir is dappled white, a similarly disruptive device.

A spiny coat

UP TO 5,000 SHARP, STIFF SPINES, sticking out at all angles, are enough to put off most predators. The spiny coat is the main defense of the Western, or European, hedgehog, a familiar mammal in the gardens, hedgerows, parks, and woodlands of Europe. Each spine is a hair changed during evolution into a sharp, stiff spike about 1 in (2.5 cm) long. The hedgehog's behavior has evolved together with its spines, so that when in serious trouble it rolls into a ball shape and waits for danger to pass.

As danger passes the head and front legs emerge

3 ALL CLEAR
The hedgehog has decided that the main threat is over and now is the time to leave. Its head straightens and is first to come out of the ball, so that the animal can smell, hear, and see clearly. Also beginning to emerge are its front legs. The hedgehog has surprisingly long legs, usually hidden under its mantle of spines. It can run well, burrow, clamber over low walls, and swim when it needs to.

Hedgehog cautiously begins to unroll

2 CAUTIOUS PEEP
The spines physically frighten the enemy, and they also act as a springy cushion should the hedgehog be pushed down a slope or against a tree. After a few moments of calm, the hedgehog relaxes slightly and peeks out of its prickly protection. Its eyesight is relatively poor, but its sense of smell is keen, and vibrations in the ground made by a creature moving nearby are felt by way of the spines.

Fully rolled hedgehog has no vulnerable parts

1 ALLOVER PROTECTION
In the face of danger, the hedgehog quickly tucks in its head, legs, and tail, and arches its back into a U-shape. A "cloak" of muscle under the loose skin pulls itself down over the head, sides, and rear. A band of muscle running around the edge of this cloak contracts, acting like a drawstring to pull the mantle of spines together around the underparts. The spines are automatically raised in the process. This defensive behavior produces the tight ball that presents nothing but spines to the molester.

DEADLY ENEMY
The fox hunts many smaller mammals, including hedgehogs. It may poke and prod at a tightly rolled hedgehog for some time in an attempt to make the animal uncurl and run off, whereupon the fox claws at the vulnerable belly.

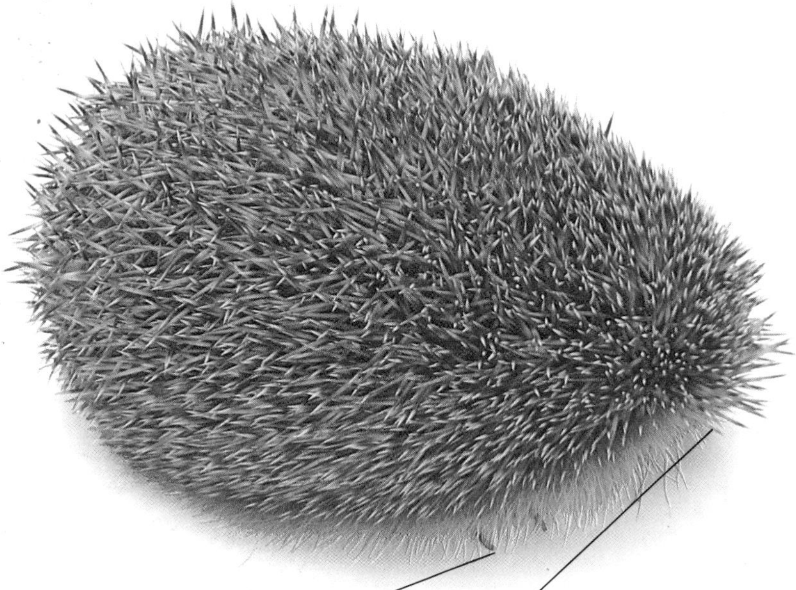

Feet barely visible

Head remains tucked under

STRANGE BEHAVIOR
Hedgehogs have often been seen to chew something foul (such as the dead toad, left), and then flick and spit their frothy saliva over their spines. It is not clear why. One theory is that this self-anointing is part of the animal's defense, helping to deter predators.

BABY'S DEFENSE
A baby hedgehog's first coat of rubbery spines lies flat under its skin at birth, but pops up within a few hours. The baby cannot roll up until it is 11 days old. Its main defense is to jerk its head upwards, stabbing predators on the nose.

4 FLIPOVER
If the hedgehog continued to unroll while lying on its back, its vulnerable underparts would be exposed to any predators. To prevent attack, the hedgehog executes a quick flipover maneuver to land on its belly, keeping its feet tucked in and its head well down for continued protection.

Head emerges to investigate surroundings

5 PREPARING TO MOVE OFF
If there is no sign of renewed threat the hedgehog uncurls further. Its head emerges to reveal which end is which, and, sniffing and with whiskers quivering, it looks around for a suitable place of safety, preferably a dark tangle of brambles and undergrowth.

6 QUICK EXIT
Defense gives way to escape, and the hedgehog scurries off to safety. This animal can move surprisingly fast when at risk - at about the speed of a human's quick walk - with its body held off the ground. But when foraging peacefully for slugs, worms, insects, and fallen fruit, it shuffles flatly among leaves and vegetation.

HEDGEHOG RELATIVE?
The echidna of Australia and New Guinea has a coat of defensive spines similar to the hedgehog's. Yet it is only distantly related, having evolved the same system of defense separately. The hedgehog gives birth to live young; the echidna lays eggs (p. 31).

Hedgehog moves quickly to safer place

Designs for defense

MANY MAMMALS have defense strategies that deter attackers without the risk of bodily harm to either. This is important when members of the same species compete for food or territories or mates. Physical signs include the displaying of dangerous-looking horns or antlers, baring of teeth, raising of fur to make themselves look bigger, and making loud sounds. Physical encounters are a risk: if the victor is wounded, although an animal might win the fight for a mate, it could then be attacked by a predator and lose the fight for life.

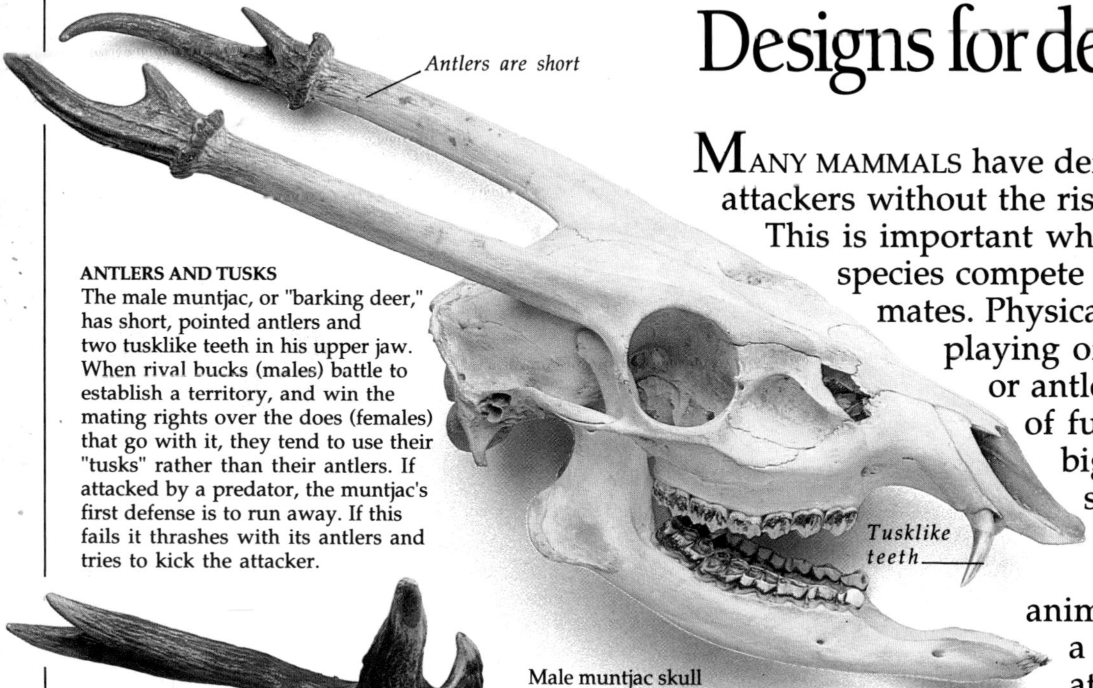

Antlers are short

Tusklike teeth

Male muntjac skull

ANTLERS AND TUSKS
The male muntjac, or "barking deer," has short, pointed antlers and two tusklike teeth in his upper jaw. When rival bucks (males) battle to establish a territory, and win the mating rights over the does (females) that go with it, they tend to use their "tusks" rather than their antlers. If attacked by a predator, the muntjac's first defense is to run away. If this fails it thrashes with its antlers and tries to kick the attacker.

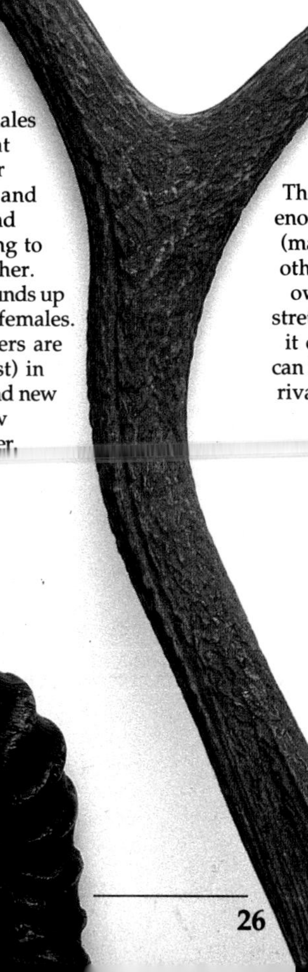

Red deer antler

Tine (point of antler)

Red deer stags fighting with antlers

CLASH OF THE ANTLERS
The impressive bony antlers of the red deer stag are a visual signal of his strength and dominance. When it comes to the autumn rutting (mating) season, they become physical weapons. Two rival males first roar and bellow at each other, then lower heads, clash antlers, and strain backward and forward, each trying to outpush the other. The winner rounds up a harem of females. The antlers are shed (lost) in spring and new ones grow in summer.

Indian blackbuck horn

Spirals in horn

Ridges on horn

SPIRALED SWORD
The horns of gazelles (the one shown here is from an Indian blackbuck) are not shed each year, like a deer's antlers. Young males fence with their horns, practicing for when they are fully mature and ready to challenge for a territory, and so for females, and so the ability to breed.

A fearsome yawn

Hippopotamus tooth

A FEARSOME YAWN
The hippo's yawn reveals its enormous teeth. When two bull (male) hippos yawn at each other they are displaying for ownership of a territory - a stretch of river or lake shore. If it comes to a fight, the teeth can inflict severe wounds on the rival, but a hippo's skin heals surprisingly quickly.

The lion and the unicorn defend a coat-of-arms

PLATED FOR PROTECTION
The armadillo resembles a mammalian tank, with its bony scutes (plates) of armor covered by horn. The scutes develop from skin, and even the tail is armored. Only some of the 20 armadillo species can roll up into a ball. An alternative defense is to "dig in" to protect the softer, vulnerable underparts.

Larger hairy armadillo

NO ENTRY SIGN
The three-banded armadillo (left) is able to roll itself up completely, while the pink fairy armadillo (below) digs a hole in which it hides. Its armored bottom acts as a barrier, rather like a cork in a bottle.

Three-banded armadillo

Pink fairy armadillo

PLAYING DEAD
Opossums have an extraordinary habit of pretending to be dead when seized by a predator, hence the phrase "playing possum." How the trick works is not clear; perhaps some predators who do not feed on already dead animals just lose interest.

ROOF TILES
The pangolin's protective scales over its body are like the overlapping tiles on a roof. This toothless ant-eating mammal has a long, scaled wraparound tail, and when it curls into a ball it is completely protected. Some types of traditional Chinese warrior armor copied the pangolin's design.

Scales from giant pangolin

The pangolin - a very unmammal-like mammal

Black rhino horn cut in half

NO DEFENSE AGAINST THE GUN
The word *rhinoceros* means "horn-nose, " and there could be no better name for the second largest of land mammals. These are museum horns, collected many years ago from an African black rhino. Today rhinos are rare, and some species are on the edge of extinction, as people still kill them for their horns - made into dagger handles or "medicines" that are in fact useless.

Crested porcupine quills

STRIPED SPEARS
The porcupine's sharp quills detach easily. When in danger a porcupine will run backward into its attacker and leave quills sticking into its skin.

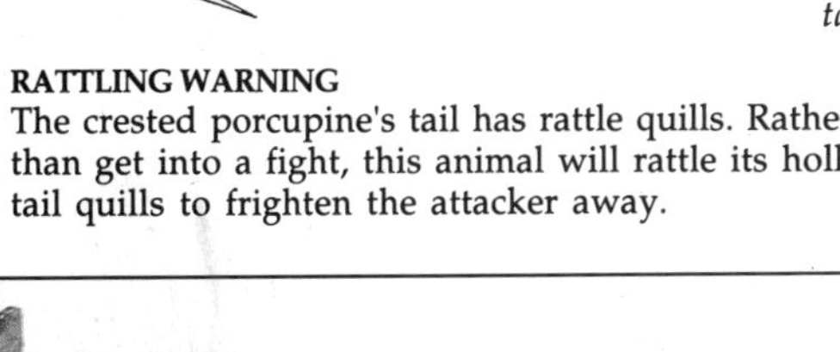

RATTLING WARNING
The crested porcupine's tail has rattle quills. Rather than get into a fight, this animal will rattle its hollow tail quills to frighten the attacker away.

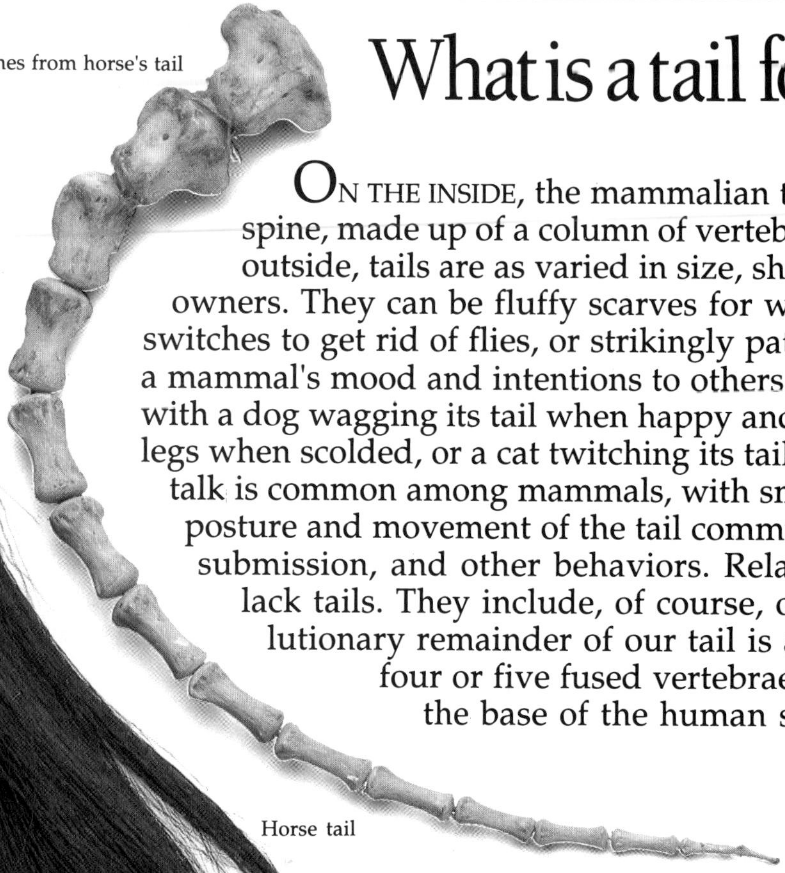

Bones from horse's tail

What is a tail for?

On the inside, the mammalian tail is a continuation of the spine, made up of a column of vertebrae (backbones). But on the outside, tails are as varied in size, shape, and function as their owners. They can be fluffy scarves for winter warmth, whisks or switches to get rid of flies, or strikingly patterned flags that convey a mammal's mood and intentions to others. Most of us are familiar with a dog wagging its tail when happy and lowering it between its legs when scolded, or a cat twitching its tail when annoyed. Tail talk is common among mammals, with small variations in the posture and movement of the tail communicating aggression, submission, and other behaviors. Relatively few mammals lack tails. They include, of course, ourselves. The evolutionary remainder of our tail is a small knob of four or five fused vertebrae, the coccyx, at the base of the human spine.

Horse tail

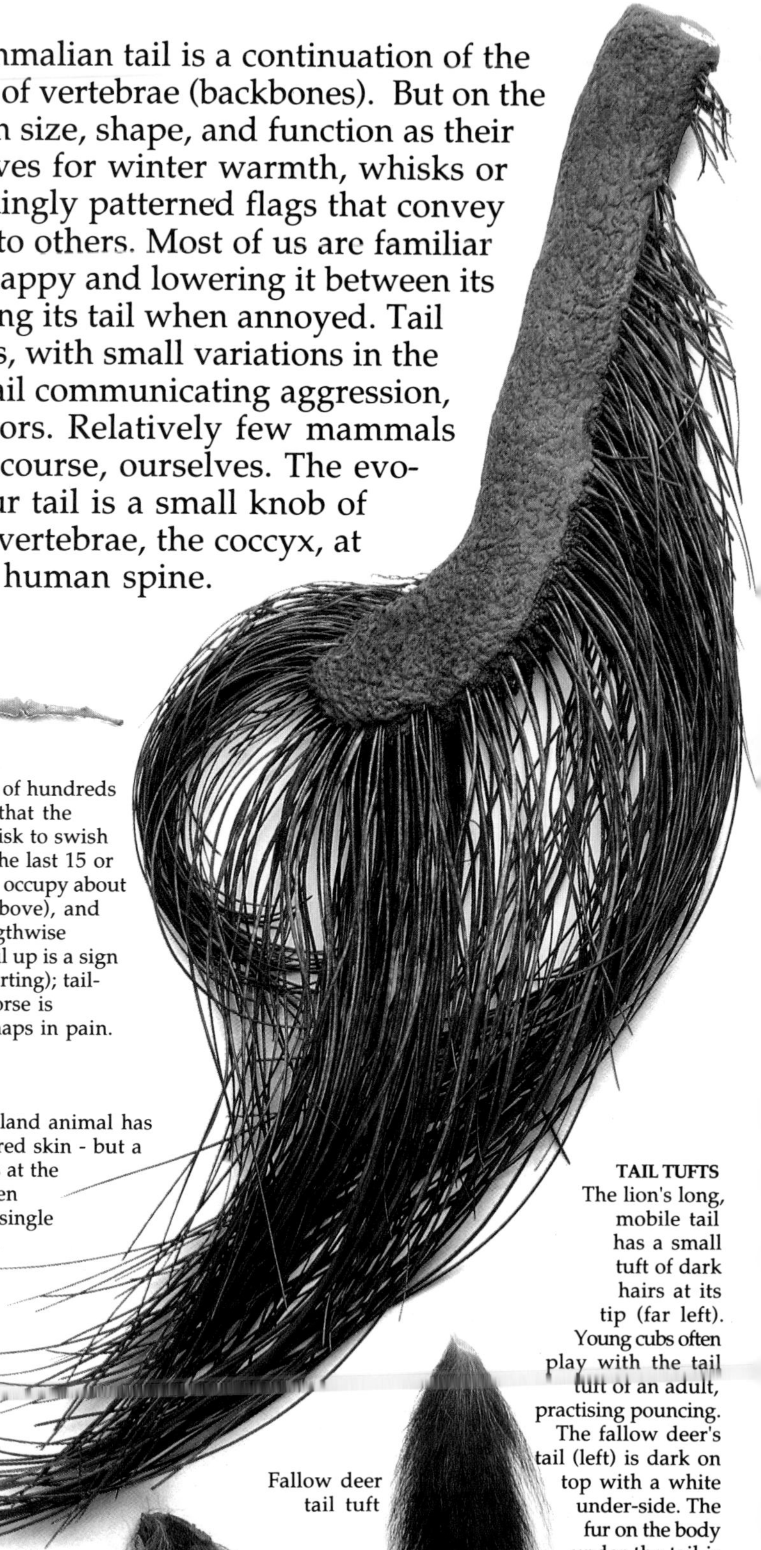

Elephant tail

HAIRY FLY WHISK
The horse's tail is made of hundreds of long, thickish hairs that the animal uses as a fly whisk to swish away irritating pests. The last 15 or so vertebrae of the spine occupy about half the tail's length (above), and these are moved by lengthwise muscles. Holding the tail up is a sign of arousal (as when courting); tail-lashing indicates the horse is angry, irritated, or perhaps in pain.

TRUNK TO TAIL
The largest living land animal has thick, sparsely haired skin - but a comb of wiry hairs at the end of its tail. When elephants walk in single file, each may curl its trunk around the tail of the one in front.

Lion tail tuft

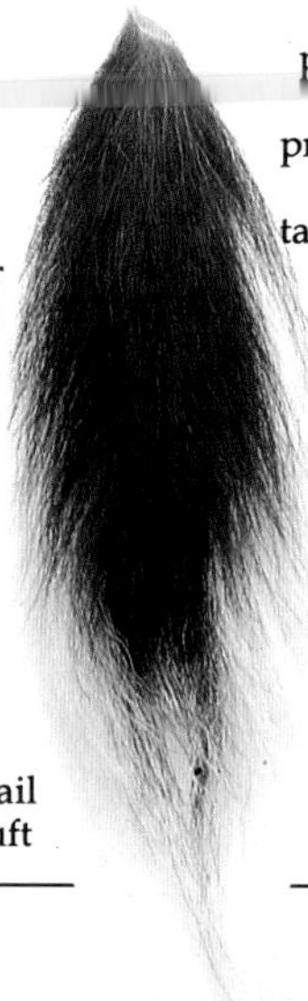

Fallow deer tail tuft

TAIL TUFTS
The lion's long, mobile tail has a small tuft of dark hairs at its tip (far left). Young cubs often play with the tail tuft of an adult, practising pouncing. The fallow deer's tail (left) is dark on top with a white under-side. The fur on the body under the tail is also whitish, with black stripes. When danger threatens the tail is held erect, which flashes a visual warning to other deer in the herd.

ROUGH FOR GOOD GRIP
Possums are marsupial tree dwellers from Australia and Southeast Asia. This tail of a New Guinea possum shows the bare, scaly skin on the underside at the tip. The rough skin gives a better grip than furry skin. The possum's tail is prehensile - able to wind around branches and function as a fifth limb (see below).

HANGING AROUND
The spider monkey has a muscular prehensile tail - a good safety feature for life spent in the trees of South American rain forests.

New Guinea possum tail

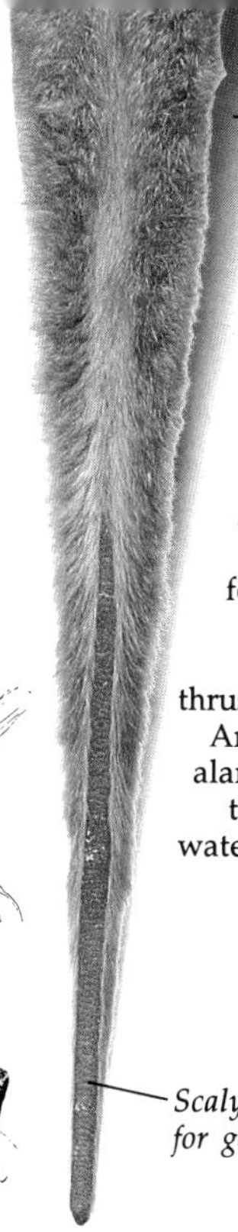

Scaly skin for good grip

Canadian beaver tail

RUDDER AND ALARM
The Canadian beaver's flat, scaly tail is used as a rudder when the animal swims with its broad, webbed back feet. The tail can also be flapped up and down to give extra thrust in an emergency. And if the beaver is alarmed, it slaps its tail down on the water surface with a loud smack to warn its companions.

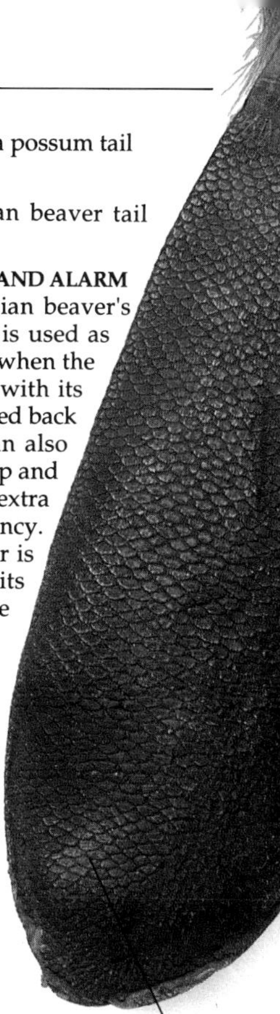

Large scales on tail

BUSHY BRUSH
The furry "brush" of the red fox makes an excellent wraparound warmer to keep the animal snug during winter. It was once thought that foxes were solitary hunters. Now it is known that they are social animals, and use their tails to give visual signals to others in the family group. The tip or tag may be dark or white.

Red fox tail

Position of scent gland - this has a role in social communication

White tag

Ring-tailed lemur tail

BLACK TIP
The stoat's winter white coat (brown in summer) is good camouflage in the snow. Yet its tail-tip remains black. It is now thought that this may confuse predatory birds such as owls, which will dive at the black tip, rather than the vulnerable head of the stoat.

RAT-TAILED
The black-tailed tree rat has the unfurry, scaly tail typical of rats and mice. The tail is used as an aid to balance.

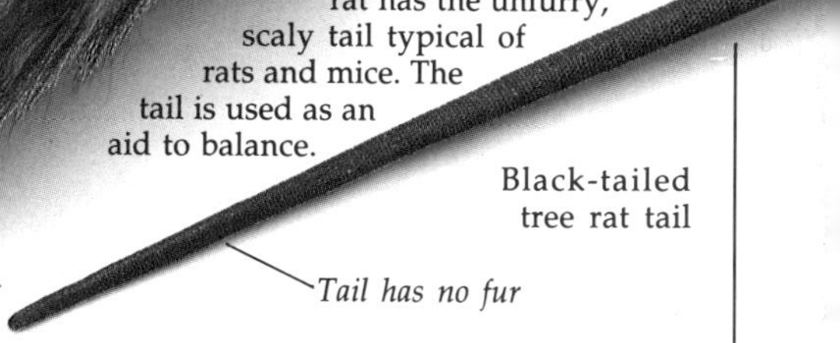

Black-tailed tree rat tail

Tail has no fur

PLATED FOR PROTECTION
Even the armadillo's tail is well armored, like the rest of its upper body surfaces (p. 27). The tough, horny plates develop from hardened skin.

Armadillo tail

Horny plates

SMELLY FLAG
Ring-tailed lemurs are social mammals, active by day and spending less time in the trees than other species in the lemur group. As they walk on all fours, their distinctive banded tails are held up in the air. When challenging other males for a ranking in the group, a lemur wipes its tail over scent glands on its shoulders and forearms and then flicks the tail over its head, spreading the scent into the air.

Banding acts as visual signal to other lemurs

THE TAIL OF THE WHALE
The muscular tail is made of two large flaps or flukes. The swimming power comes from the muscles in the back moving the flukes up and down.

Horsfield's flying squirrel tail

TAIL FOR FLYING
The flying squirrel swoops from tree to tree, parachuting on flaps of skin on the sides of its body. The flattened tail acts as a rudder and an air-brake.

Flattened to help with steering

An early birth

Australian marsupials

MOST MAMMALS DEVELOP in their mother's womb (uterus). When born they are well formed, and in many species they are up and about within hours of birth (p. 35). Pouched mammals, or marsupials, don't follow this system. What sets them apart from all other mammals is the way they reproduce. The Eastern gray kangaroo is a typical example: its baby grows for only five weeks in the womb. When born it is just 1 in (2.5cm) long, naked, blind, and unrecognizable as a kangaroo (see opposite). It wriggles from the birth opening (which is not the same as the birth canal of other mammals, p. 35) to the teat (nipple) in the mother's pouch. As it takes the teat in its mouth and sucks, the teat swells and the baby is "stuck" there as it continues to grow and develop. The pouch, therefore, acts as a sort of external womb where the baby continues its development. After a while the baby's jaws enlarge and it can let go of the teat. Later it grows enough to leave the pouch for short periods. After about 10 months the youngster is too big to get into the pouch.

Four-month-old male red-necked wallaby

Adult female red-necked wallaby

KANGAROOS AND WALLABIES
This mother red-necked (or Bennett's) wallaby with her joey (baby) is a typical member of the kangaroo and wallaby family. There are about 50 species in the family, out of the 120 or so marsupial species found in Australia. There is no real difference between a kangaroo and a wallaby: larger species tend to be called kangaroos, and smaller ones wallabies. The scientific name for the family is Macropodidae, which means "big feet." This reflects the way they move - bounding along in great leaps on the huge feet, using the tail as a counterbalance. Some large kangaroos can travel at 40 mph (nearly 65 km/h). When grazing on plants (all kangaroos and wallabies are herbivorous) they move slowly, resting their tails and front paws on the ground as they swing the back legs forward. At rest, they sit back on their tails or lie lazily in the shade of a tree. The red-necked wallaby was one of the first marsupials seen by Europeans, when the British First Fleet anchored in Sydney Cove in 1788. Its traditional name is the "brusher," since it prefers brush and wooded areas rather than more open country. The four-month-old joey is now beginning to leave his mother. But at the first sign of danger he hops back to the safety of the pouch. He leaves the pouch at nine months, but will not be weaned (p. 33) until about 12 months old.

After its epic journey to the pouch, the developing kangaroo attaches itself to the teat and suckles milk (p. 36), just like any other mammal

An even earlier birth

Only three of the 4,000 or so mammal species lay eggs. These are the platypus of Australia, the short-beaked echidna of Australia and New Guinea, and the long-beaked echidna of New Guinea. They are the only members of the Order Monotremata (p. 8), the egg-laying mammals. When the white, leathery-shelled eggs hatch, about two weeks after laying, the young feed on mother's milk. The milk oozes from enlarged pores on to the skin, where the babies drink it; monotremes have no teats (p. 36).

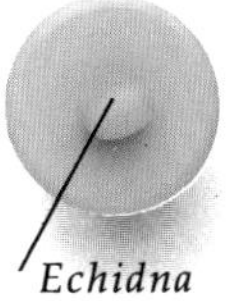

Echidna egg

Platypus head

Echidna head

MARSUPIAL MONKEY?
Some opossums - marsupials of the Americas - look rather like monkeys; but they are not closely related except by both being mammals. This woolly opossum lives in the tropical forests of Central America and northern South America. Like a monkey it has large, forward-facing eyes, to judge distances accurately as it moves through the branches. It also has a prehensile tail, like some South American monkeys. It is a fruit and nectar feeder, like many monkeys. Yet its breeding is typically marsupial. After birth, the babies hold on to the teats in the pouch continually. As they grow, they are able to clamber around on their mother and get a ride.

LOST FOR EVER?
The thylacine, or Tasmanian tiger, is a striped, wolf-like marsupial. Or rather it was, since it is probably extinct. The last captive thylacine died in 1936 in Hobart Zoo, Tasmania. From 1938 these creatures were protected by law, having been hunted for their raids on sheep and poultry. Possible sightings are reported now and again in Tasmania's wild hill country, and even on mainland Australia, but many naturalists believe this marsupial has gone forever.

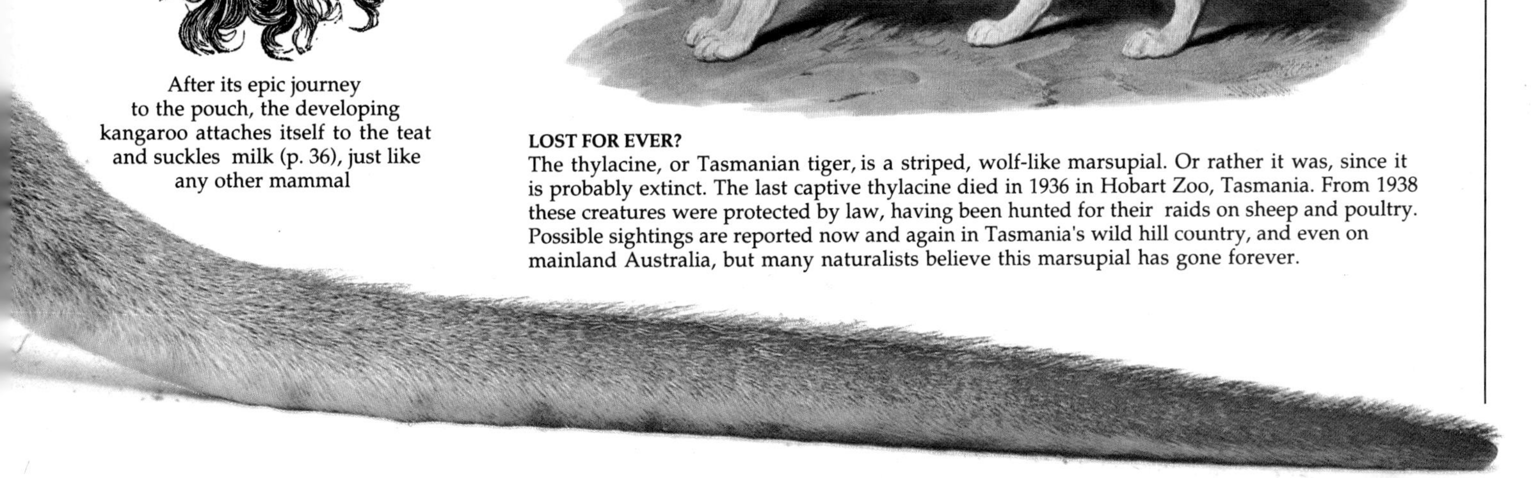

Fast breeders

MICE ARE SMALL, relatively defenseless mammals. They are easy prey for many other creatures. Their strategy for survival is to breed at an extraordinary rate. A female house mouse starts to breed when she is six weeks old and can have up to 10 litters in a year, with about five to seven babies in a litter. If all the young survive and breed in turn, one pair of mice may become half a million mice!

1 BIRTH DAY
The mouse mother has built a cozy nest of woven straw, grass, moss, and other plant pieces. Around human habitation, house mice may use bits of shredded cloth, burlap, or paper. The nest is made in a safe place such as down a hole, under floorboards, or behind a wall. About 20 days after mating, the mother gives birth. The babies are barely recognizable as mammals, let alone mice - pink, hairless, earless, and blind - and are totally dependent on their mother.

2 TWO DAYS OLD
The wriggling, rubbery babies divide their time between taking milk from mother (suckling, pp. 36-37) and resting in the cozy lining of the nest. Their tails are lengthening and their eyes and ears are becoming more prominent.

RETURN OF THE WANDERER
The mouse is a good mother. She locates babies who wriggle or fall from the nest, partly by following their squeaks, and will carry them by mouth back to safety.

3 FOUR DAYS OLD
After two more days, the babies are beginning to resemble mice. Their ear flaps are visible and their limbs and feet have taken on more mouselike proportions. They make squeaks audible to us and also ultrasonic squeaks, too high to be heard by the human ear. The mother can hear them, of course. If she leaves the nest for too long and the babies get cold, they will call to her ultrasonically, as if asking "Please come and warm us up!"

SIGN OF THE MAMMAL
Feeding the young on milk is a unique mammalian trait, and the mother mouse feeds her babies regularly. This gives them the energy they need to grow at such an amazing rate.

4 SIX DAYS OLD
The youngsters take on a house-mouse brown as their fur appears. This is a risky phase, since their movements and their squeaks are becoming more forceful, and so their nest is in greater danger of being found by prowlers. The mother continues to suckle; her offspring will not be weaned (off milk and onto solids such as seeds and grains) until they are about 18 days old. The father is long gone. He takes little or no part in family life.

5 TEN DAYS OLD
The eyelids are now open and the young mice can see, although they are nearsighted creatures. They are also more mobile, with increasingly coordinated movements. In many mammals, the young would have reached this stage of development in the womb, and they would now be born (see the kittens on pp. 34-35). However, mice rely on large litters to keep up their numbers, so the young are born in a premature state, since the mother would be unable to carry so many big babies in her womb.

6 FOURTEEN DAYS OLD
The mice are now becoming curious about their surroundings and leave the nest for short periods. In a few more days the young mice will be ready to make their own way in the world. Soon they will face hazards alone, such as predators, lack of food, exposure to the elements - and overcrowding as they themselves begin to breed.

Nine lives

A MAMMAL WHOSE BABIES DEVELOP INSIDE THE MOTHER'S WOMB is known as a placental mammal. The womb protects the babies until they are fairly well developed. A special organ called the placenta supplies the baby with food and oxygen. Cats are placental mammals and the babies are born with all their fur. Compare the kittens with the baby mice on page 32 (also placental) and the baby wallaby on page 30 (a marsupial). In many species, the gestation period (the length of time it takes for the baby to develop in the womb) is linked to body size. In shrews it is about two weeks; in rhinos, 16 months. The birth itself is a dangerous time for mother and babies, since they are unable to flee and the smell of the birth fluids may give them away. Birth is generally a private affair, and even group-dwelling mammals such as deer leave their companions for a safe spot in which to bear young.

About to be born

Amniotic membrane emerging from birth canal - kitten is inside this

One kitten has already been born

1 THE WAITING IS OVER
After nine weeks' gestation, the time for birth has arrived. This domestic cat is too busy to mind the lights and camera. She has her favorite rug and this is her second litter so she knows exactly what to do. In the wild most mammal mothers hide in a den sheltered from the wind and rain - the babies could easily die of exposure. When it is time for birth, the mother's womb contracts (becomes smaller), and the babies are pushed down the birth canal into the outside world. As each kitten emerges, it is still inside the amniotic membrane, or sac, which enclosed it in the womb.

The moment of birth

Amniotic membrane has broken

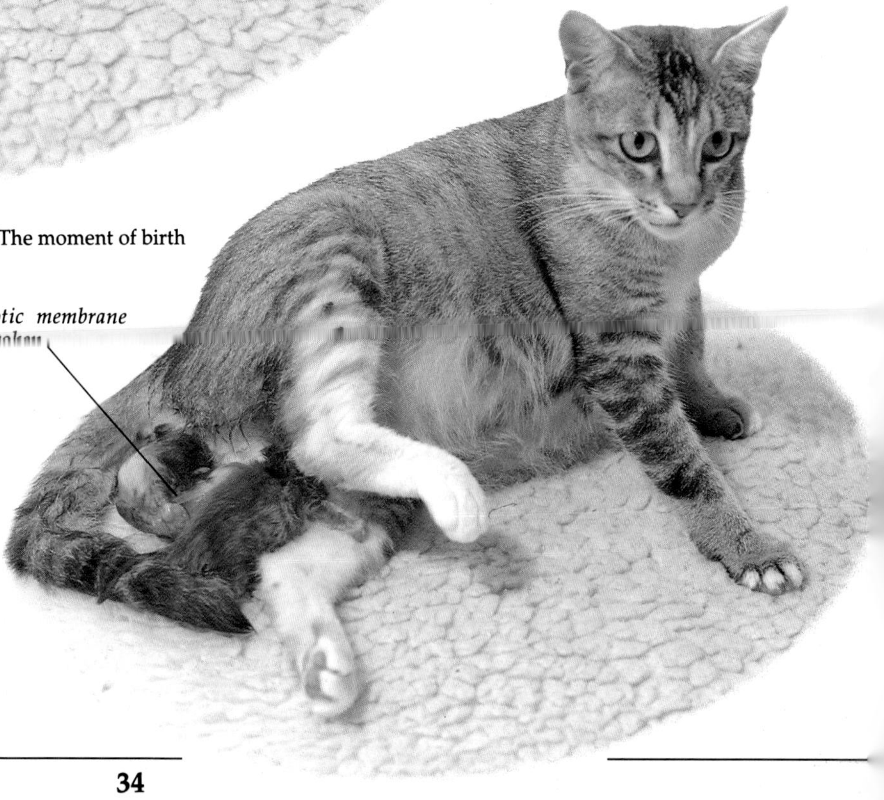

2 FIRST BREATHS
In the womb, the developing mammal receives oxygen and food from its mother by way of a special organ called the placenta, which is in the inside wall of the womb and looks like a piece of liver. In the placenta oxygen and food pass from the mother's blood to the baby's blood. The baby is attached to the placenta by a "lifeline" called the umbilical cord. At birth, the placenta comes away from the wall of the womb and, still attached to the baby by the umbilical cord, follows it along the birth canal and emerges shortly after the baby (this is why the placenta is sometimes called the afterbirth). The baby must then start to breathe for itself. As soon as the amniotic membrane is broken (by the birth, or bitten by the mother), the fluids drain away, and the baby gulps its first breaths of air.

3 CUTTING THE CORD

The kitten waits by the mother's tail until the placenta comes out. During the wait, the blood in the umbilical cord clots and prevents the kitten from bleeding to death when the mother chews through it. The mother will then eat the placenta, as it is a good source of nutrients at a time when she cannot get out to feed. Also, its odor would attract unwelcome attention from predators and flies if she did not clean it up. After this the mother licks the kitten, drying its fur so that it fluffs up and keeps the baby warm. In the meantime, the first-born kitten has scrambled along its mother's body, using smell and touch to find her teats to suckle milk (p. 36). It is hard work for the mother - as the kittens are born within about half an hour of each other there is always one to be licked and cleaned. In the wild, the mother cat will fiercely attack any animal that dares to interrupt her at this time. Even her kittens struggle and spit if threatened. The domesticated mother cat appreciates help and attention from a trusted human, but her kittens hiss and bare their toothless gums like wild kittens if they smell someone near them.

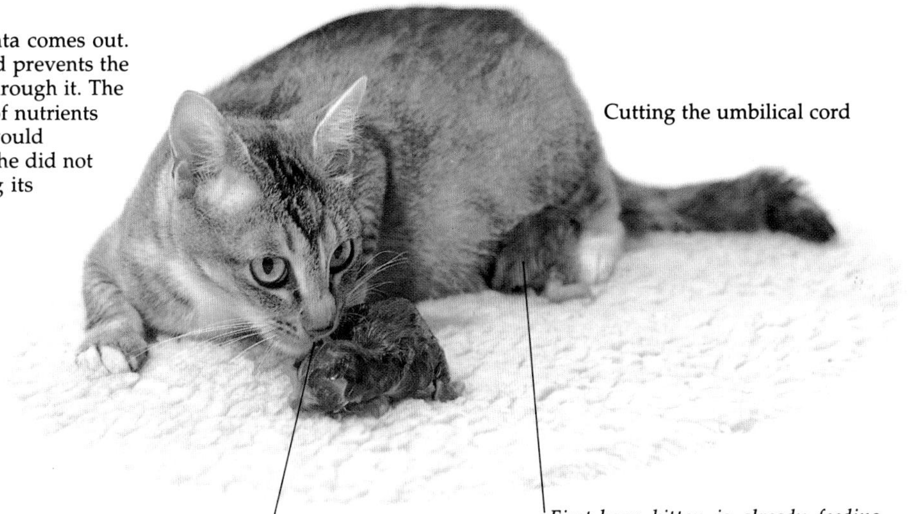

Cutting the umbilical cord

First-born kitten is already feeding

Mother uses her teeth to cut the umbilical cord

A heap of brothers and sisters

4 IT'S HARD WORK BEING BORN

The damp newborns look squashed and tired after their birth. Their eyes and ears are sealed, so they are blind and deaf, but they are not as helpless as they might seem. In fact, they are very active and they are built to last. If the mother accidentally sits or steps on them, they squeak vigorously and let her know about it.

UP AND ABOUT

Unlike the defenseless kittens, a newborn calf is soon able to walk and run. Evolution has insured that hunted animals, especially in open habitats, spend as little time as possible giving birth.

5 HAPPY FAMILY

The kittens have all been born. It was a large litter, but the births were quick and easy, with no problems for the mother. She continues to lick and dry all the kittens repeatedly. Soon she will be able to lie back and sleep while the kittens suckle contentedly, dry and warm against her belly. The riskiest time is over.

Unique to mammals

A mare has two teats between her back legs. She nudges her foal toward them; the foal then feeds on average about 4 times each hour.

THE MAMMARY GLANDS, unique to the mammalian mother, form in the skin. They resemble specialized sweat glands and grow in two milk lines on each side of the abdomen. Cats and dogs have several glands and teats along each side; in hoofed animals they are near the hind legs. In primates (including humans) they are on the chest, a site that may be connected with adaptation to a tree-dwelling life and the consequent need to hold the babies with the forelimbs. During pregnancy, the mammary glands increase in size under the influence of the female hormones estrogen and progesterone. Milk production is stimulated by another hormone, prolactin. After birth a hormone called oxytocin, from the pituitary gland (just under the brain), causes the gland to release its milk and encourages formation of more milk. Milk is the young mammal's complete food, providing even the water it needs.

The mother cat (p. 34) with her third, much smaller, litter

THE NEAT TEAT

Unlike kittens, puppies usually feed from whichever teat they can find. The teat is a rubbery-textured lobe of tissue. It fits neatly inside the baby's mouth, to minimize loss of milk as the baby suckles. The teat also acts like a shut-off valve to prevent leakage of milk after feeding.

CONTENTED CAT AND KITS

Within an hour of birth, a kitten is suckling (sucking milk from its mother's teat). Since there is usually about 20 minutes between the births of successive littermates, and there are four or five kittens in an average litter, the first-born will already be suckling when the later ones arrive. The tiny kitten, although unable to see or hear, can smell - and can feel with its whiskers, fur, nose, and feet. It moves to the milk supply by scrabbling with its feet, first locating the warmth of the mother's body, then working its way along until it finds a teat. It kneads the teat with its feet and face, to stimulate milk flow. After an initial free-for-all, each kitten tends to settle into a routine and suckle from its own teat. If there is a large litter, the young may feed in shifts.

Newborn kittens feeding on their mother's milk

MATERNAL MANATEE
The manatee, a marine mammal, has teats situated just behind her front flippers, near her "armpits." The youngster feeds underwater, lying by its mother's side in calm water. Sometimes the mother holds the baby with her flipper to keep it from floating around in water currents, a bit like a human mother cradling her infant.

THE WOLF TWINS
The legendary founders of ancient Rome, human twins Romulus and Remus, were supposedly suckled by a she-wolf until discovered and raised by shepherds. It is unlikely that wolf's milk could provide the nutrients required by humans.

SEARCHING FOR THE NIPPLE
A human baby, unlike many other mammals, loses weight slightly after being born but regains birth weight by one week. In the "rooting reflex," when the baby's cheek is stroked it turns to that side, searching for the nipple - a useful, built-in behavior for a newborn.

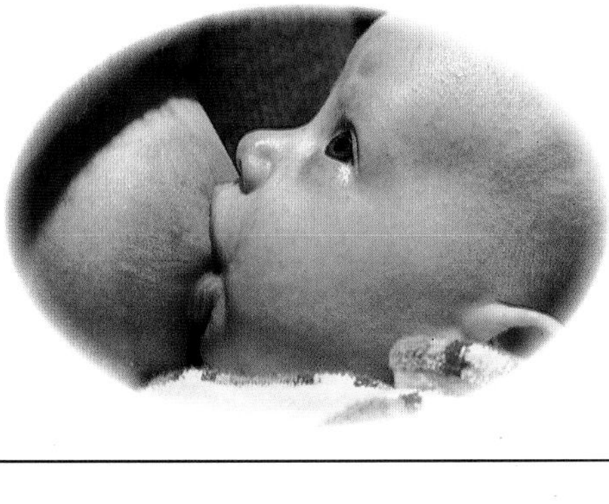

Growing up

COMPARED TO OTHER ANIMALS, mammal parents invest a lot of time and energy in their young. An insect may lay hundreds of eggs and leave them to their own devices. A sea urchin casts thousands of eggs into the water and has nothing more to do with them. Mammals adopt a different strategy. In general, they have only a few offspring, but they look after them well. The young are cleaned, fed, kept warm, protected, taught, and generally cared for until they are self-sufficient. The degree of parental care varies, however, within the mammal group. We are at one end of the spectrum: human parents spend many years raising their children. The mother tree shrew is at the other end - she leaves the young in a nest after birth and returns only once every couple of days. The female cat looks after her kittens until they are weaned and old enough to feed themselves. Kittens grow rapidly, as these pictures show, getting the energy they need for growth from their mother's milk (p. 36). By nine weeks old the kittens have grown enough to leave their mother. Compare this with the wallaby (p. 30) and the mice (p. 32).

HELPLESS AT SIXTY-THREE DAYS OLD
While the young cat has become self-sufficient, a human baby of the same age is relatively helpless. One of its most rewarding behaviors is to smile, which encourages affection and handling (and so warmth) and strengthens the mother-baby bond. But it will be many more years until it is fully independent.

Newborn kitten

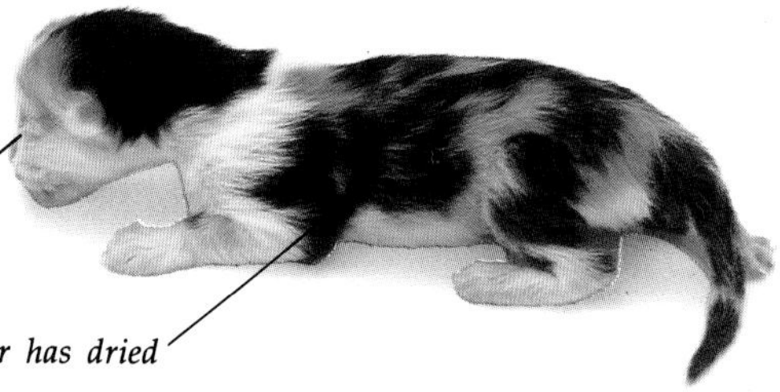

1 BIRTH DAY
Kittens have their fur at birth. But living in the watery environment of the womb makes the baby look waterlogged. The water is amniotic fluid. (p. 34). The mother licks her offspring thoroughly and the fur is soon dry and shiny. The kitten is relatively helpless: it cannot see or hear (the eyes and ears are closed), and it cannot lift its head. But it can feel and smell, and push itself along, so that it soon finds the mother's teat and begins to feed (p. 36).

Seven-day-old kitten

2 SEVEN DAYS OLD
In a week, the kitten has doubled its weight from the 3.5 oz (100 g) or so at birth. Its eyes are just beginning to open. They cannot yet detect colors and shapes; these are just a jumble at first. The kitten must learn to recognize and make sense of what it sees, and this takes time. The mother cleans it and licks up urine and feces. In the wild this is sensible behavior, because a soiled and smelly nest would soon attract predators.

Twenty-one-day-old kitten

3 TWENTY-ONE DAYS OLD
By now the kitten's eyes and ears are functioning well, and it can hold its head up. Its weight has quadrupled since birth, muscles are now stronger and more coordinated, and the legs are a bit longer, so that the youngster can just about creep along in a shuffling manner. If the kitten is in trouble it mews loudly, showing the first or "milk" teeth that appear between the age of two and three weeks.

Thirty-day-old kitten

4 THIRTY DAYS OLD
After feeding, the kitten's abdomen hangs down and only just clears the ground, since its legs are still relatively short. By now it is walking confidently and leaves the nest of its own accord to explore and play. One great change is the process of weaning: the kitten is starting to sample solid food and suckle less milk from the mother. She brings prey back to the nest and allows the kitten to examine it, so that it learns what it should hunt later.

Face is changing proportions and looks less babyish

Kitten can stand

Forty-two-day-old kitten

Head is still large in proportion to body

5 FORTY-TWO DAYS OLD
By six weeks of age, the kitten still has a large head and shortish legs, but its general body proportions are becoming more like those of an adult cat. It now leaves the nest for longer periods, exploring and playing with its littermates (domestic cats average about five kittens to the litter). Coordination is increasing and the kitten can run, jump, and climb, though it rarely ventures far from home. Solid food features more in the diet, but much nourishment still comes from the mother's milk. A female lemming of this age would already be pregnant with her first litter.

Sixty-three-day-old kitten

Tail is longer - more adult-like

6 SIXTY-THREE DAYS OLD
Most kittens are fully weaned by nine weeks. Although still part of a family, enjoying each other's company, they are now able to fend for themselves and could be separated from the mother. The young cat seems very playful but much of its activity has the important function of teaching it how to catch prey and avoid danger (p. 42). This tortoiseshell youngster, playing with red wool, is training its eye-paw coordination, sharpening its reactions, and testing the grip of its claws - as well as finding out about the wool when this is caught.

Not a natural object, but the baby orang could be learning to manipulate a ripe fruit

The game of life

IT IS DIFFICULT TO IMAGINE an ant or a leech playing. What we humans call play seems fairly restricted to mammals, with their well-developed senses and ability to learn and to be intelligent. Play occurs chiefly in young mammal It is generally an unserious business, seemingly carried out for its own sake, with none of the purpose found in adult behavior patterns such as feeding or establishing a territory. Young chimps chase in a rough-and-tumble, badger cubs roll and frolic on the forest floor, and even baby platypuses waddle around, squealing and yelping like puppies. Theories about why young mammals play are not in short supply. For the individual, it helps to develop strong muscles and good coordination. For survival, it trains a carnivore in hunting techniques or a herbivore in detection of and flight from threat. For social mammals it provides a basis in communication, in the use of sounds and body posture to send messages of dominance and submission that coordinate the group. Do adult humans play? Probably, but we use different words. Sports, hobbies, and pastimes are sometimes called "play."

Testing the strength of the fabric

THE CHIMP AND THE CLOTH
This two-year-old male chimp was allowed to play with a strip of cloth. He had seen fabrics before, but this new piece deserved some general attention to appreciate its color and gauge its texture and strength (left) - and, as always, to test the faint possibility that it might be good to eat. Next came a series of actions to wear the fabric. The chimp watched his human companions closely while doing this. When the result got a response from them, usually laughter at the cloth becoming a "scarf" or "hat" (above) or a face cover (far right), he was encouraged and experimented further. Later, he turned his attention to details and began studiously to unpick individual threads from the fabric (below). Many aspects of future behavior are seen here, from arm-muscle strength needed to build a leafy bed each evening, to the refined finger skills required when grooming (p. 44) or feeding on small food items (p. 49).

Concentrating to unpick threads

Using the fabric as a hat

NO TERMITES HERE . . .
In the wild, chimps eat mainly fruits and leaves. But they also take termites and ants from holes, using sticks as tools (p. 49). Hole-examining is a common behavior and occurs in situations that we might consider strange. Finding juicy termites in the hole on the base of a toy building brick is highly unlikely. But, for the chimp, you just never know. . .

TOY TIME
We are so used to watching human babies playing with educational toys that we may lose sight of the evolutionary origins of such activity. In many groups of people with less industrialized ways, sticks and stones and leaves make ideal natural toys.

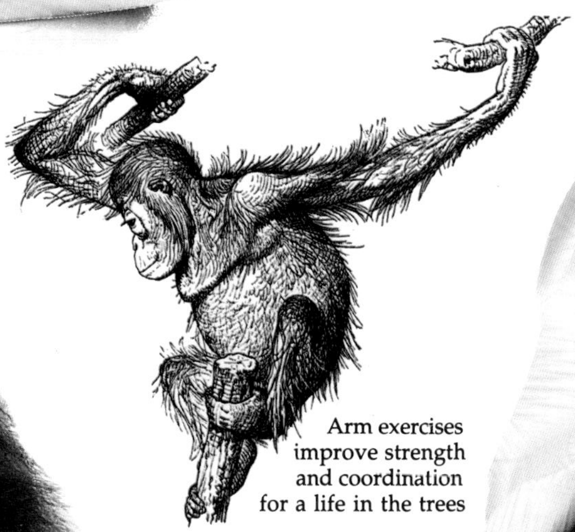

Arm exercises improve strength and coordination for a life in the trees

Using the fabric as a face-cover

Playful dolphins: these very social marine mammals seem to follow ships for fun.

...continues

PLANT-EATING MAMMALS may have to travel and search to locate food, but once found, the plant is relatively easy to "catch." For the hunting carnivore (meat eater), finding food is more risky. It involves much effort, stalking, or tracking prey. When it comes to the kill, there is a risk of injury from the victim's defenses (p. 26). If the prey escapes, time and energy has been wasted. So it is not surprising that the play of young carnivores, such as cats and dogs, appears to mirror so many features of adult hunting life. To prevent misunderstanding and accidental injury, it is important that the animal wishing to play conveys this fact to its fellows; otherwise they might take its actions seriously. A puppy will make a "play bow," crouching down on its chest, rump and back legs up, tail wagging and ears pricked forward, in a posture that says: "Let's play!" Human children have their equivalent - a giggle that takes them into the world of make- believe.

Feline funtime

Many of a playing kitten's actions can be interpreted in terms of the hunting techniques used by the adult cat. Kittens play on their own, testing themselves, and also in a group, pretending to be the hunter or the hunted.

SWAT
Midair swipes require good eye-paw coordination if they are to connect with a moving target. This type of movement is made as a hunting cat claws a low-flying bird or clouts a mouse that has leaped into the air.

TEASE
Even some adult cats "play" with a small animal before finally killing it. The squeaks of a captive shrew or flutterings of a grounded bird seem to provide entertainment, but the significance of this behavior is not clear.

SCOOP.
The kitten tries to put its paw, sole up, under the ball and pick it up or flip it over. The ball does not turn over and so intrigues the animal. Adult cats scoop up small prey, including fish, using this type of movement.

POUNCE
The "mouse pounce" is one of the most characteristic cat actions. Other hunters use it too, such as the fox. The aim is to come down suddenly and silently on the victim's back, away from its teeth and claws, and then, before it has time to resist, sink the teeth into its neck. In this case, the mother's tail acts as the mouse.

Who's the boss?

Dogs - wolves, jackals, dingos and all domestic dogs - are mostly pack animals. Puppies playing together gradually develop many of the social signals they will use when adult, to keep the pack organized.

MAN'S BEST FRIEND
Most dogs behave toward their owners much as they would toward a dominant member of their pack.

TESTING TIME FOR TEETH
The brown puppy, playing on his own, is biting and gnawing the ring as though it were a bone, testing teeth and strengthening jaw muscles.

TUSSLE BETWEEN THE TWO
The black-and-white puppy appears on the scene and wants to join in the game. The two brace themselves and pull hard. This type of action is seen in many pack hunters when they work together to bring down a large prey such as a deer. It may also occur when two animals are competing for a piece of the prey.

TAIL-BITING
The tug-of-war goes on until the bigger brown puppy gets the ring from his brother but, having got the toy, he soon tires of it and bites his brother's tail instead. They are still playing, but the bite is hard enough to mean business.

I'M THE BOSS!
The puppies now romp together, snarling and biting in a noisy playfight. Suddenly the black-and-white puppy nips too hard. The brown puppy gets mad and the play turns into a power struggle. Muzzles wrinkle, teeth are bared, and the puppies glare at each other. The stronger brown pup stays on top to show who is the boss. The black-and-white puppy rolls on his back as a sign of submission to his stronger brother.

Keeping clean

THE MAMMAL'S FURRY COAT is fine for keeping the animal warm and dry. But it is a dirt trap, and a paradise for parasites, which feed on shed skin or the nutritious blood flowing just beneath. Licking, scratching, combing, shaking, wallowing, bathing, rubbing, picking, and nibbling are some of the techniques that mammals use to maintain personal hygiene, reduce the risks of disease, and ensure any wounds are kept clean as they heal. Many animals clean themselves, but social grooming, where one individual cleans another of the same species, is widespread among mammals. Social grooming has several functions. One of course is cleanliness: a helper can more easily reach those awkward places such as the neck and back. Another is social organization: dominant individuals may demand to be groomed by lower-ranking ones. Grooming also spreads the group's scent to all members, allowing them to identify each other and pick out intruders.

YOU SCRATCH MY BACK . . .
Social grooming in baboons not only keeps these mammals clean, it also establishes each animal's position in the group.

ATTENTIVE MOTHER
Young mammals cannot clean themselves, especially baby rodents, which are born naked and helpless (p. 32). This mother hamster is licking her offspring clean. Its fur must be kept clean and dry; if it gets damp, the fur lies flat and cannot trap body heat, which for such a small animal means rapid cooling and the risk of hypothermia (lowered body temperature).

The neck and top of the head are cleaned by the front paws

Paws can reach difficult places

Teeth are used to "comb" fur

NOT A "DIRTY RAT"
Even a "dirty" animal such as a rat spends much time grooming its fur and cleaning its skin. Rats kept domestically are exceptionally clean and make fine pets. The teeth act as a comb to unsnag and brush out the fur, and teeth and claws scratch off lice and dead skin. Wild rats do carry parasites, especially fleas. In 1346-49, rat fleas that bit humans spread the bacteria that caused the bubonic plague - the Black Death - in which perhaps half the people in Europe died.

The rat finds a safe, quiet place in which to groom - it does not want to be caught by a predator. It reaches around to its back and flanks, cleaning by nibbling and combing.

DUST BATH
Some mammals, such as elephants, use the "dry-shampoo" technique, also employed by many birds to keep their feathers in tip-top condition. This is the dust bath, where dust is kicked or thrown onto the body and then rubbed and scratched and shaken, to dislodge dirt and loosen clinging parasites. The chinchilla maintains its luxurious fur in this way, there being plenty of dust in the rocky Andes Mountains of South America. Time and energy spent grooming is worth it: the fur protects the chinchilla from the bitter mountain cold and wind.

Long, deep fur

Chinchillas rolling in dust bath

The underparts, which rub the ground and pick up dirt, are cleaned by the mouth and front paws (compare the cat's method of grooming on the next page)

Rat bends double to clean its underside

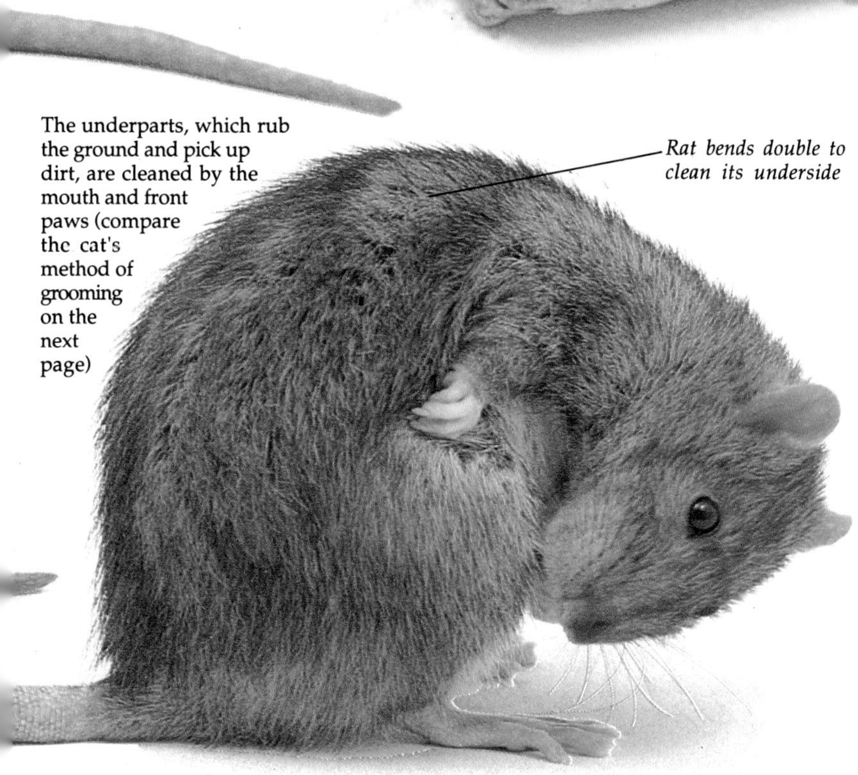

HELPFUL FRIEND
Creases in the rhino's thick skin are ideal hideaways for ticks and other parasites. The tickbird helps its huge host by picking out and eating the parasites. The bird gets a meal, the rhino receives a cleanup - a biological relationship called symbiosis.

At the cat wash

Many people are fascinated as to why the typical domestic cat seems to have so much time to clean itself. It is partly because the pet cat has no real need to spend time hunting - food is provided. Cats may groom when they have nothing better to do. They also groom as a "displacement activity." A cat that has pounced and missed a bird may sit and wash itself, allowing the awkward situation to pass.

TWO HORSES ARE BETTER THAN ONE
Mutual grooming in horses helps remove lice and ticks from difficult-to-reach parts such as the withers (shoulder point) and top of the tail. One horse can scratch and rub itself on a favorite post but a helper improves efficiency. One horse approaches the other, mouth slightly open to signal a grooming session. The pair then stand neck-to-neck or head-to-tail and nibble each other for 5-10 minutes. In a herd, horses develop special grooming friends.

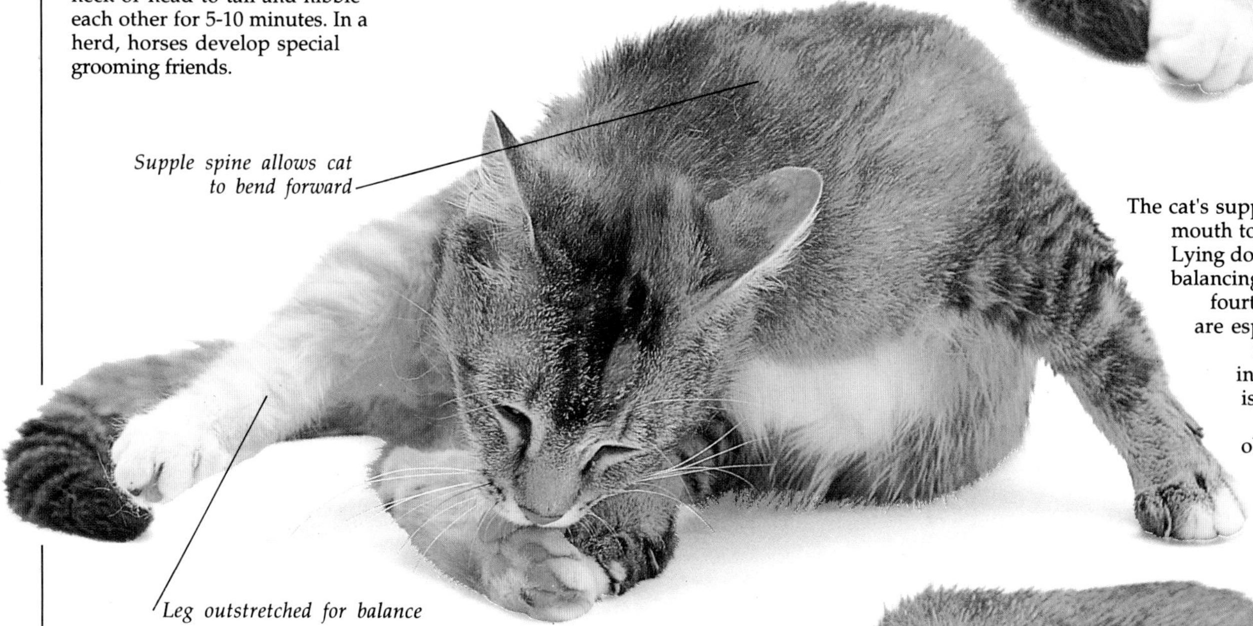

Supple spine allows cat to bend forward

Leg outstretched for balance

U-TURN
The cat's supple, agile body allows its mouth to reach most parts easily. Lying down is more relaxing than balancing on three legs while the fourth is being washed. Paws are especially important, since if they become injured or infected the cat's mobility is reduced, and with it (in the wild) the ability to obtain food. The sole pads are freed of dirt and the claws exposed and examined to check for still-stuck bits of prey.

THAT SHOW-RING SHINE
Horses remove parasites and loose hair themselves, but human preference at the horse show is for a squeaky-clean coat that outshines the competition. Horses probably judge each other on different points.

Front paw moistened with saliva used to clean behind ears

THE FACE RUB
Many mammals (including humans) lick their lips after a meal to clear bits of food from around the mouth. The rest of the face cannot be reached so easily by the all-important tongue, which carries saliva that moistens and removes dirt. So the cat licks saliva onto its front paw, and wipes and rubs the paw over neck, ear, eye, and whiskers to clean them.

PAW LICK
People who have been licked by a cat recall the harsh, sandpaper-rough tongue, with its tiny papillae (bristles). The human tongue bears these, but they are less stiff and brushlike. The tongue "combs" the fur, while the cat's small incisor teeth work like tweezers to nibble and pick off broken and loose hairs, dead skin, clinging dirt, and parasites. As grooming continues, the cat becomes more contented and relaxed. The front paws are usually "washed" toward the end of the session, since they have been used to clean other areas, such as the face.

REAR-END ACCESS
This is one of the most characteristic poses of a cleaning cat, with one leg held up in the air to gain access to the abdominal and anal areas. Any bits of feces and dampness from urine are removed.

THE END RESULT
One clean cat. The fur is still slightly damp from saliva, but it soon dries and fluffs up. Grooming helps to spread waxy and oily skin secretions over the skin and hair, forming a semi-waterproof barrier that repels germs. Frequent use of strong shampoos tends to wash these natural secretions from human hair. Mammals should be clean, but not too clean!

How to deal with a meal

Three-course meal: house mice make short work of cream, bulbs, and candle wax during their nightly trips to the kitchen.

A LARGE, COLD-BLOODED ANIMAL such as a snake may go for weeks without eating. But mammals, being active and warm-blooded, need lots of energy to keep them going. Energy, as well as the raw materials for growth and reproduction and body maintenance, comes from food. Feeding is therefore vital to life. In modern society, humans spend relatively little time hunting for food. It may take what seems like all day to go around the supermarket, but we have lost sight of how most wild mammals build their daily routine around finding enough to eat. One of the reasons for the mammal's high energy requirements is the ability to be active in cold conditions, when the cold-bloodeds are chilled and slow. This may be why much mammalian food-hunting is done at dawn and dusk, before the heat of the day allows reptiles, insects, and other cold-blooded prey to warm up and dart away. The smaller the mammal, the more feeding it has to do, since small bodies have proportionally more surface area than large ones, and so lose heat at a greater rate. In cooler climates, the smallest mammals have only just enough hours in the day to feed themselves. Shrews do little else except feed in a frenzy, then rest and digest, then feed again. They eat their own body weight in food each day, and can starve to death in only three hours. At the other end of the meat-eater scale, the lion needs only the equivalent of about 1/40th of its body weight in food each day. Mouths and teeth give evidence as to the types of food eaten (p. 50); claws are also good clues (p. 58).

TREE-TOP TONGUE
The giraffe's long, dark tongue stretches upward to add another 1 ft (30 cm) or so of height to this tallest of land mammals. Vegetation more than 20 ft (6 m) high can be cropped by a large male giraffe. The tongue grasps leaves and twigs and pulls them within reach. The canine teeth have two deep grooves to strip leaves from their twigs.

Chipmunk feeding on nuts

HAND-TO-MOUTH
The chipmunk holding food in its handlike forepaws is a common sight in eastern North America. These naturally curious members of the squirrel family frequent picnic sites and parks in the hope of finding leftovers. The chipmunk handles food in a most efficient manner. As it feeds, it rotates food items quickly, scrabbling off loose bits and testing with the teeth to find the weak point where nuts can be cracked. Like many other rodents, it uses its cheek pouches to carry surplus food back to its burrow (p. 52).

GRAIN DRAINS
Apart from ourselves, house mice are probably the world's greatest graminivores (grain eaters). Even in the wild these small rodents have an amazingly varied diet and tackle seeds, fruits, leaves, shoots, and other plant matter, and also insects and other small creatures. In and around human habitation they become still more unfussy. They have eaten bread, paper, string, butter, soap, candle wax (see opposite), and other waxy or fatty substances, plus of course the famous cheese used to bait mousetraps. House mice have even been known to invade butchers' cold stores and feed on chilled or frozen meat. The mouse gnaws and chisels at the food with its long, sharp front incisors typical of the rodent group (p. 50); it usually holds small items in its front paws. Its lower incisors leave two characteristic grooves.

House mice feeding on grain

CLAWS FOR EVERY OCCASION
The Malayan sun bear, like most of its relatives (p. 50), is an all-around feeder (omnivore). It is the smallest bear, and its light weight and long, curved claws (relative to other species) enable it to climb well and also hook ripe fruit from branches. It also tears bark from trees with its claws to uncover grubs and the nests of termites and bees.

THE RIGHT TOOL FOR THE JOB
The chimp's brain takes over when its physique fails. Faced with termites deep in a strong nest, our closest relative takes a stick and dips it into the hole. The termites grab it, and the chimp fishes them out and licks off a tasty meal. A few mammals, and some birds, are known to use tools in this fashion.

FISH SUPPER
The otter rarely eats its catch in the water. It comes to the bank and holds down the slippery meal with its front feet while tearing at the flesh with its sharp, spearlike canine teeth (p. 50). Otters also eat small mammals, birds, and frogs.

Grippers and grinders

MAMMALS, being warm-blooded and generally active, need to take in plenty of food to provide sufficient energy for life. The jaws and teeth are at the forefront of feeding: they grasp the food, cut it into smaller pieces if necessary, and do some preliminary crushing and grinding before it is swallowed. The basic structure of the mammalian tooth is a soft inside containing nerve and blood vessels, overlaid by tough dentine, and covered by enamel. Yet from this simple plan, mammals have evolved a huge variety of choppers, snippers, impalers, shearers, grippers, grinders, and many other tooth shapes. Teeth are especially important in studies of mammal evolution, because they are often well preserved as fossils and so are one of the few ways of comparing extinct species with living ones (pp. 12-15).

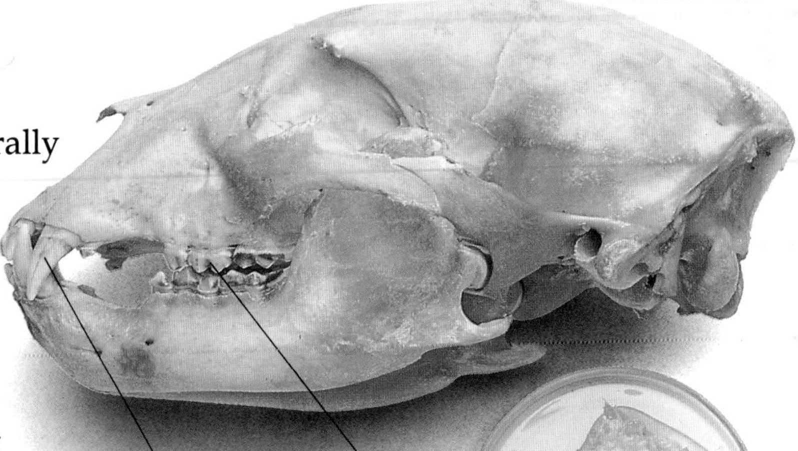

Honeycomb

Fish flesh

THE ADAPTABLE BEAR
Bears are classed in the order Carnivora (p. 8), but in reality some species eat a variety of foods in season, from fish, rodents, and young deer to buds, fruits, and berries - and the legendary honey. The bear's teeth are adapted accordingly - pointed incisors and canines for the meat and grinding molars for plant material.

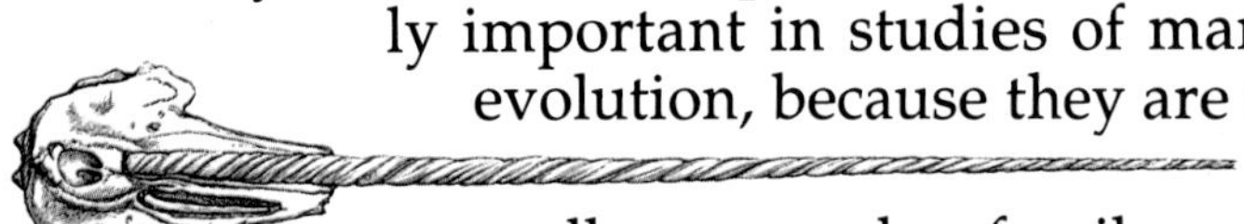

The male narwhal's 10 ft (3 m) "tusk" is an overgrown left tooth. Its function is not certain - it may be a male symbol to win over females.

PANDA PUZZLE
The giant panda has long puzzled experts. Its general body structure indicates that it belongs to the order Carnivora (meat-eaters), yet its diet is principally herbivorous - it eats mostly bamboo, although it will also eat insects, small mammals, and carrion. Recent evidence suggests that its closest relatives are probably the bears.

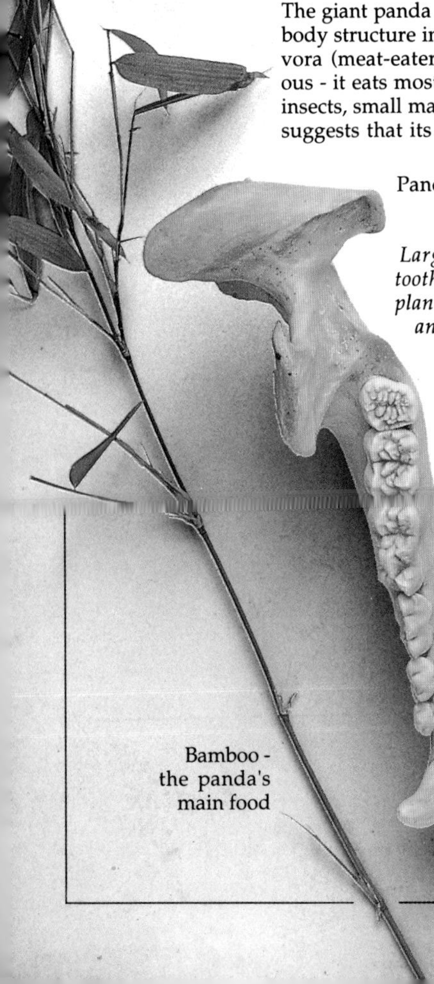

Bamboo - the panda's main food

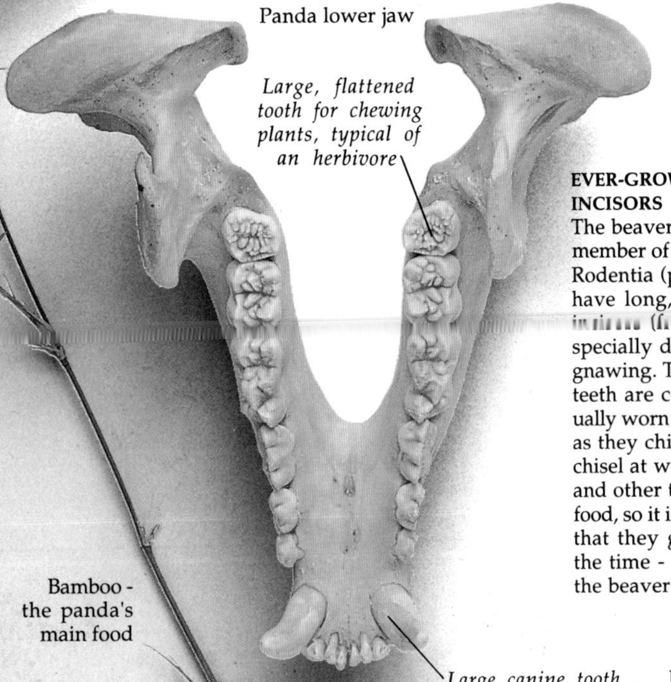

Panda lower jaw

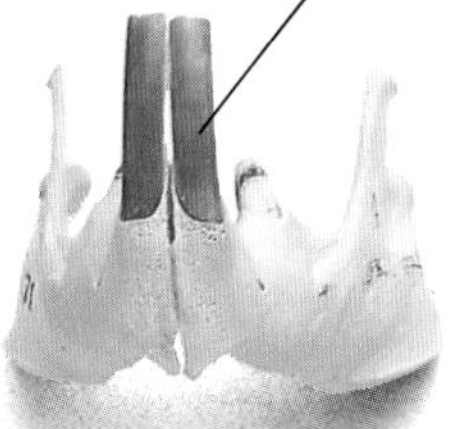

Canadian beaver lower jaw

EVER-GROWING INCISORS
The beaver is a member of the order Rodentia (p. 9). Rodents have long, chisel-like incisors (front teeth) specially designed for gnawing. These teeth are continually worn down as they chip and chisel at wood and other tough plant food, so it is good that they grow all the time - otherwise the beaver would starve.

Bark and buds - the beaver's food

MOUTHFUL OF GRASS
The horse's teeth are in two main groups. Small, sharp ones at the front (incisors and canines) work with the lips and act as croppers to snip off grass. Large, flat teeth at the back (molars) grind the nutrients out of the grass.

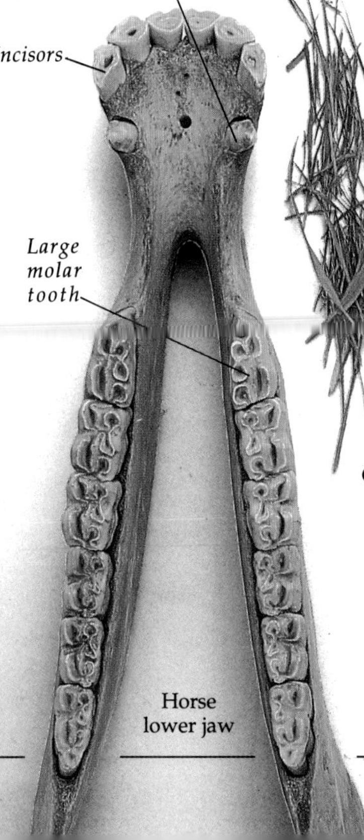

Horse lower jaw

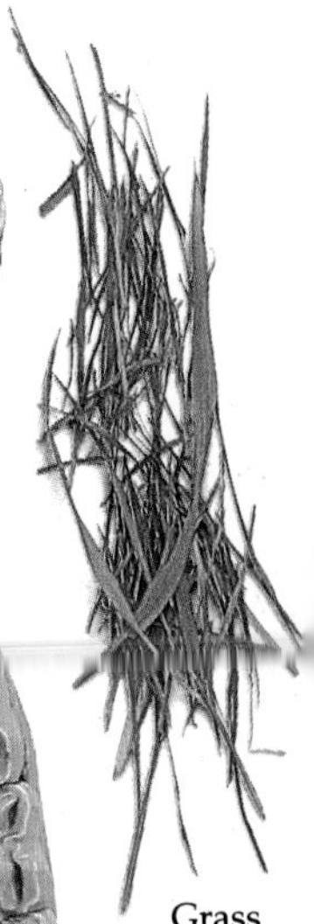

Grass

CARNASSIAL POWER

Jackals are often considered scavengers, cleaning up the leftovers at a lion's kill. But they hunt too. The ridged carnassial teeth near the jaw joint can shear skin, gristle, and bone.

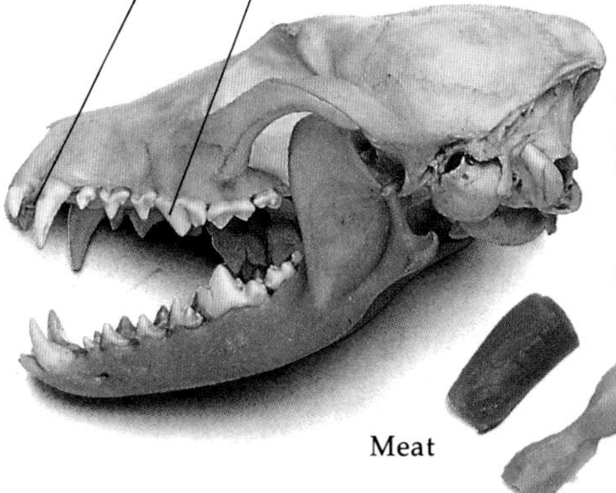

Golden jackal skull

Meat

NO TEETH

The long-beaked echidna eats small worms and insects. It has no teeth - the prey is taken in by a sticky, spiny tongue and mashed between the rough back of the tongue and the roof of the mouth.

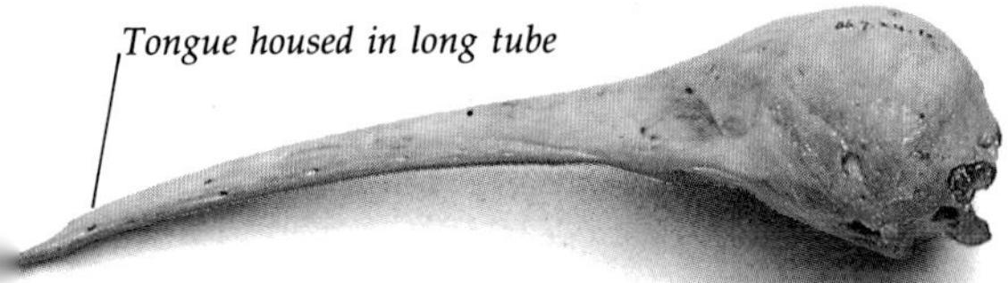

Long-beaked echidna skull

THE UNUSUAL AARDVARK

Africa's aardvark is unusual in many ways. It only has back teeth, and these have no enamel. They do little chewing, since ants and termites collected by the sticky tongue are crushed in the specialized stomach.

A tamandua (collared anteater) forages for ants and termites with its long, sticky tongue; it has no teeth (left)

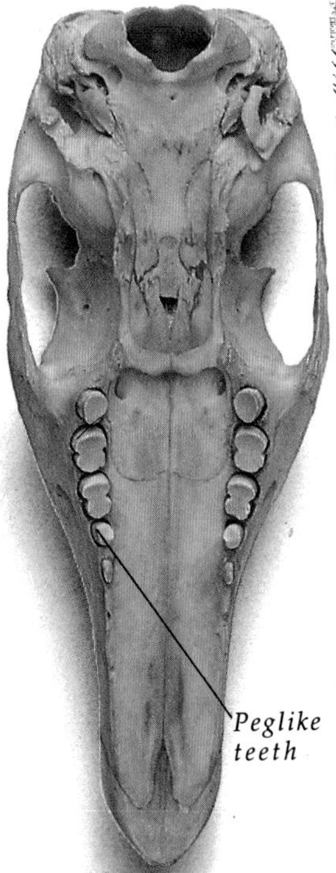

Aardvark skull from below

RAZOR SHARP

The hedgehog has small, sharp teeth to chew up its diet of caterpillars, grubs, and beetles.

Hedgehog skull

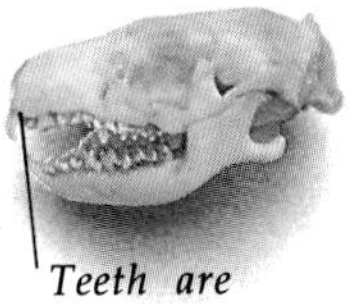

Fringed plate of baleen

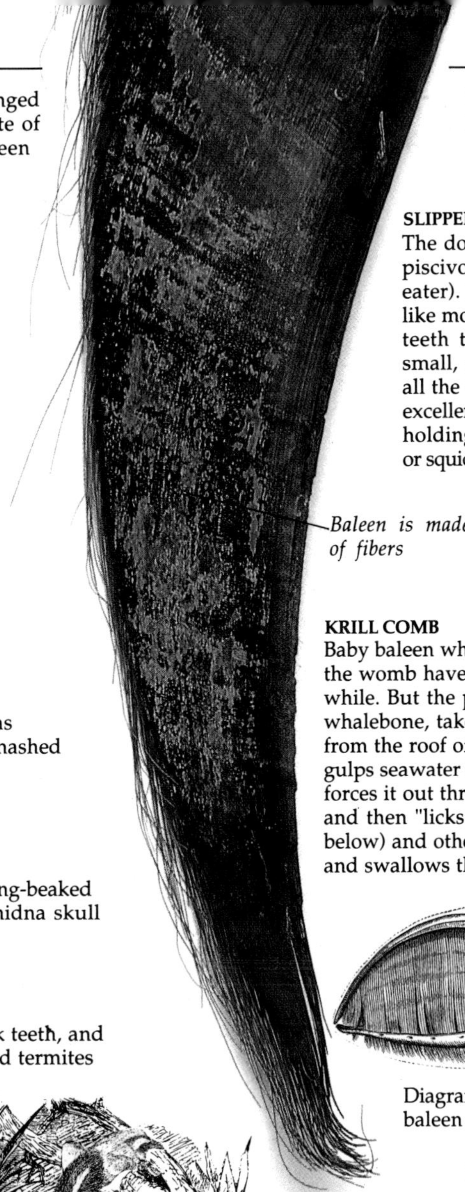

Dolphin lower jaw

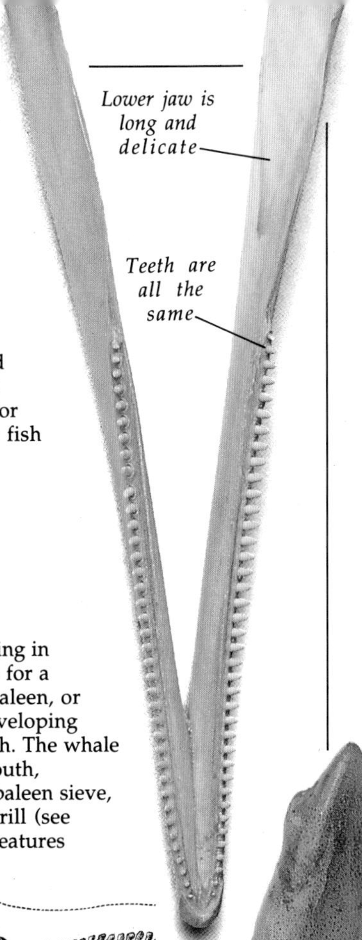

SLIPPERY CATCH

The dolphin is a piscivore (fish eater). Its beak-like mouth bears teeth that are small, sharp, and all the same - an excellent design for holding slippery fish or squid.

KRILL COMB

Baby baleen whales growing in the womb have tiny teeth for a while. But the plates of baleen, or whalebone, take over, developing from the roof of the mouth. The whale gulps seawater into its mouth, forces it out through the baleen sieve, and then "licks off" the krill (see below) and other small creatures and swallows them.

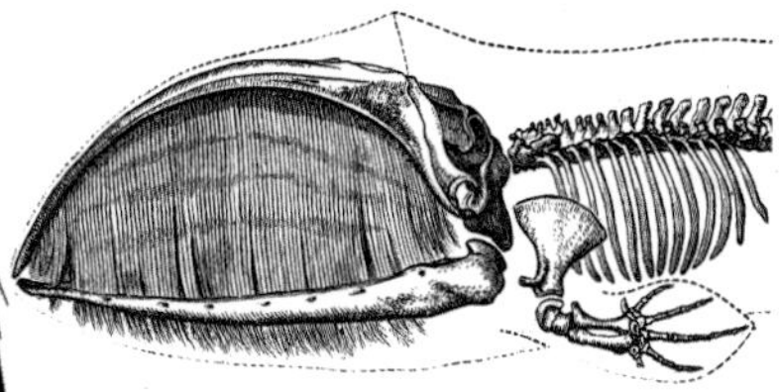

Diagram to show rows of baleen in whale's mouth

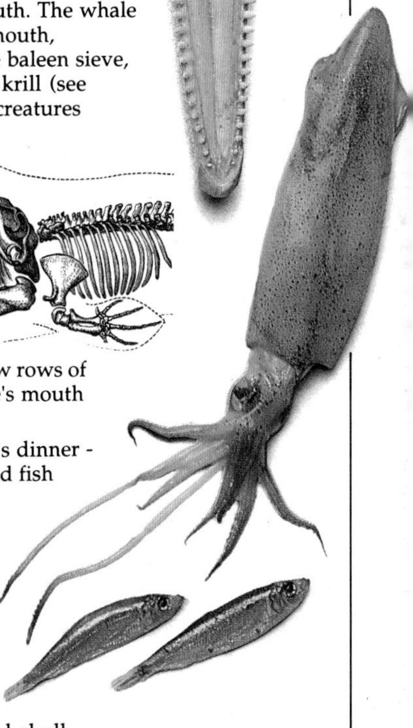

Dolphin's dinner - squid and fish

Crab-eating seal skull

THE CURIOUS CASE OF THE CRAB EATER

The crab-eating seal of the Antarctic does not actually eat crabs, it eats krill. Look closely at the intricate teeth of this seal and you will see how it can sieve tiny shrimplike krill from the seawater under the pack ice.

Krill

Food for later

FEW HABITATS IN THE WORLD provide a constant, year-round supply of food. Our distant ancestors recognized this, and they understood the need to build up a store for later. Planning ahead by planting crops and storing fruits led to the beginnings of agriculture some 10,000 years ago. Other mammals, however, have probably been saving food in times of plenty, to be eaten when times are hard, for millions of years. Seeds a favorite. In a seed, the parent plant has provided a rich store of nutrients that the embryo (baby) plant will rely on when it germinates. The seed is therefore a ready-packed, nutritious meal. In return, the seed storers help the plant. An animal that buries seeds and then forgets about them has helped the plant to spread. Meat is more of a problem, since it tends to decay, but burying is still worthwhile for mammals such as foxes. With its legendary cunning the fox does not store all its surplus food in one place. It makes several stores in different places, so that if another animal discovers one store, the fox does not lose the lot.

A cheeky way to collect food

The golden hamster is a rodent (p. 9). Like many of its relatives it collects food when this is abundant and caches it (stores it away in a hidden place). The hamster's cheek skin is loose and floppy, and forms an expandable pouch in which food is carried. A number of mammals carry food in this way, including the platypus.

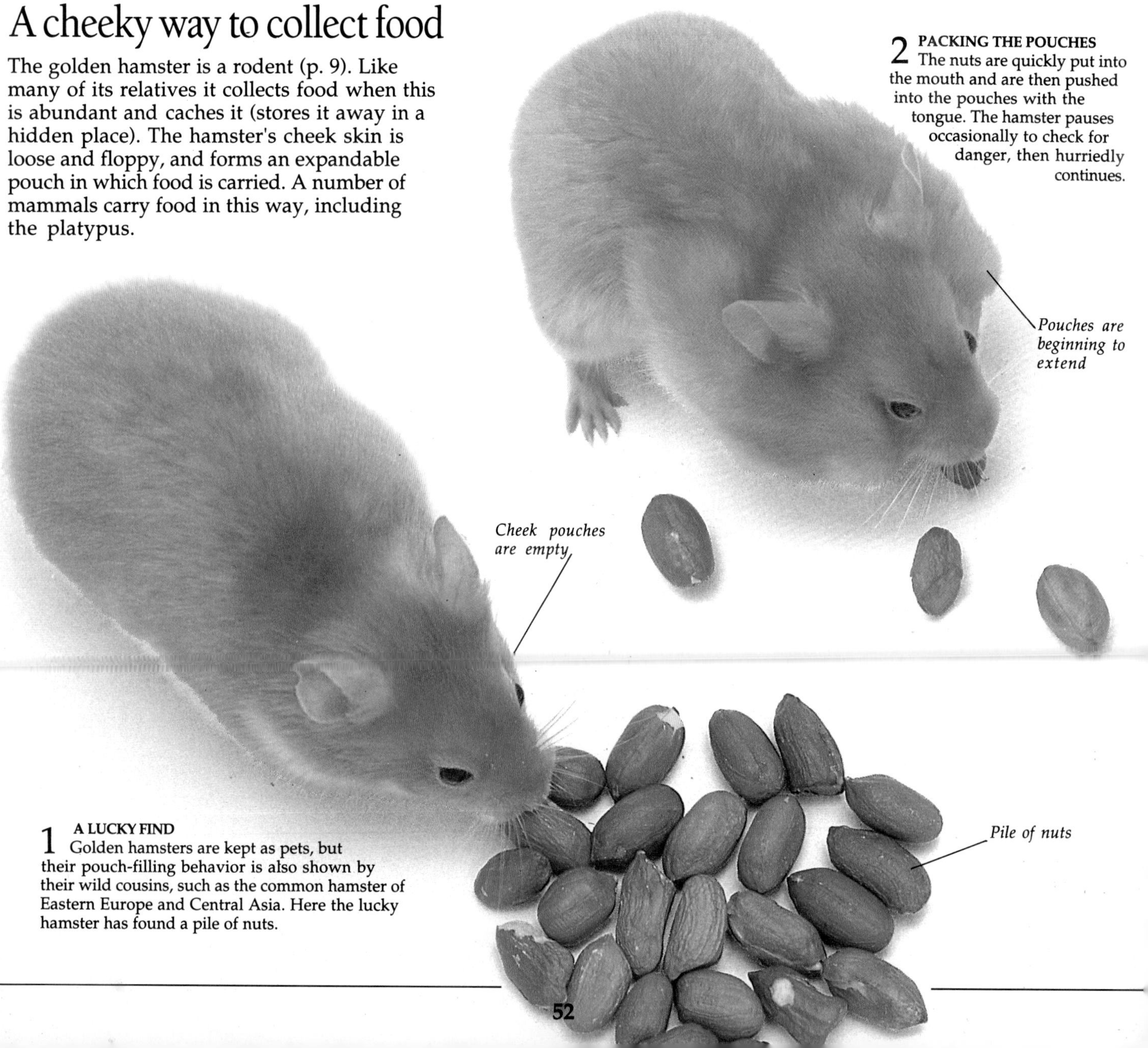

2 **PACKING THE POUCHES**
The nuts are quickly put into the mouth and are then pushed into the pouches with the tongue. The hamster pauses occasionally to check for danger, then hurriedly continues.

1 **A LUCKY FIND**
Golden hamsters are kept as pets, but their pouch-filling behavior is also shown by their wild cousins, such as the common hamster of Eastern Europe and Central Asia. Here the lucky hamster has found a pile of nuts.

Food for the future

Mammals use many different methods and go to great lengths to store the energy and nutrients that a meal represents. The methods have evolved in response to availability of food in the habitat.

PACA'S PACKAGES
The paca is a nocturnal rodent about the size of a small dog, and it lives in northern South America. Its square-headed look is due to its curved, bowl-like cheek bones, once thought to be used for storing food. In fact, their exact function is not clear – one theory is that they are used to amplify the sound that the paca makes.

Paca skull

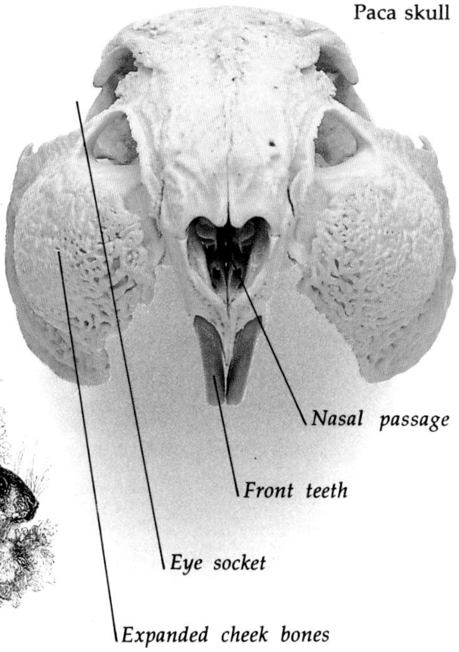

MEAL UP THE TREE *above*
The leopard is successful in only a small proportion of hunts. It cannot eat a large catch like an impala in one go, so it may store the leftovers in a tree, out of reach of hungry rivals like hyenas.

MEAL IN THE TREE
The red fox buries extra food and then returns to it later. But not always successfully - another creature may find it, or the fox may forget where it put it.

WINTER WARMTH AND ENERGY *right*
The dormouse feeds greedily on autumn fruits and builds up stores of fat under the skin. This provides enough energy for a half-year of hibernation.

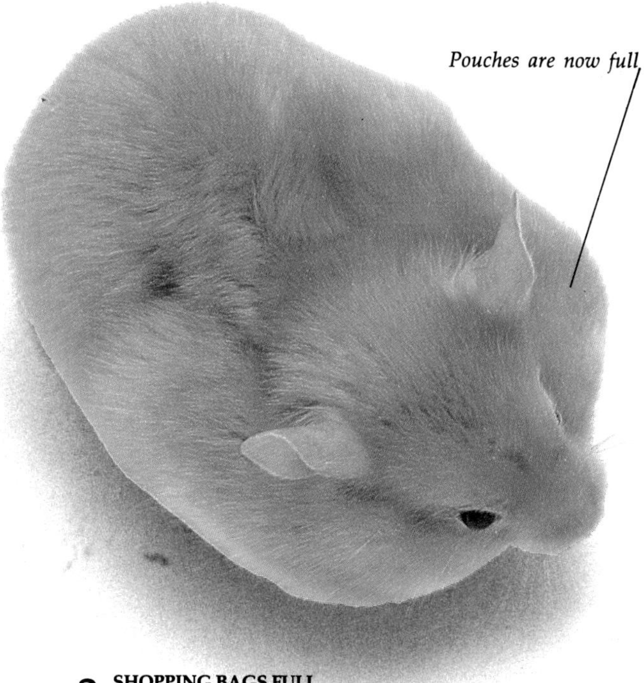

3 SHOPPING BAGS FULL
Like a human shopper staggering home from the market with a heavy bag in each hand, the hamster has packed its cheek pouches to bulging with nuts. Now it is time to leave the feeding area, which is exposed and therefore hazardous for such a small, relatively defenseless rodent.

4 FROM BAG TO BURROW
When the hamster reaches the safety of its burrow, it unpacks its pouches. The front paws are used like hands to push and massage the food out of the pouch and into the creature's underground larder. In the wild, a single hamster has been found to collect more than 132 lb (60 kg) of nuts and other food (equivalent in weight to an adult human).

At home in a nest

Harvest mouse nest built on cereal stalks.

NESTS OF VARIOUS SORTS occur throughout the animal world. We are familiar with birds' nests, and some of the busiest and most elaborate builders are insects such as termites. Mammals, too, have a fair share of species that make visible nests in the open, as well as many species that nest in burrows (p. 56). They include squirrels in Europe, pack rats in North America, karoo rats in Africa, and bandicoots in Australia. One of the most extraordinary mammalian nest-makers is the stick-nest rat, a rabbit-size native of Australia. This very rare rodent makes a strong, interwoven pile of branches, twigs, and even stones, 3 ft (1 m) high and 6 ft (2 m) across. It lives in the rocky southern lands, where digging is difficult, and the nest probably gives protection against predators. Sadly, this rat has died out on the mainland, and only an island colony remains off the south coast. It seems it was never common, and both aborigines and Europeans hunted it.

SHREDDING THE BEDDING
In the wild the gerbil, a small, desert-dwelling rodent, digs burrows away from the heat and dryness, and lines them with shredded plant matter. In captivity, the results of digging behavior may be prevented by the cage. But the animal can still make the lining if material is supplied.

DAY ONE
The raw straw that was supplied to two gerbils before they woke up in the evening.

DAY TWO
A night of shredding with the teeth produces a partly made nest.

DAY THREE
More shredding, and the nest fluffs out and takes shape.

THE GRAY IN ITS DREY
A winter walk through woodland in Europe, with trees bared of foliage, may reveal soccer-ball-size bundles of sticks wedged into the forks of trees. These are dreys, the homes of gray squirrels. Some will be old and deserted, and others will be flimsier summer dreys, not used in winter. But a few dreys will each hold an occupant like this one which, in winter, is not hibernating but probably sleeping. Squirrels are active (mainly at midday) throughout the winter and can only survive a few days without food. They stay in the winter drey at night and in very bad weather. The drey is a tangle of twigs and sticks, some with leaves still attached, and is lined with bark, grass, and other bits and scraps gathered by the owner. This drey is about 1.5 ft (45 cm) in diameter, with an internal chamber 1 ft (30 cm) across. Baby squirrels are born in special nursery dreys in spring.

Things that a drey might be made of

WHAT'S IN A DREY?
Gray squirrels tend to take any suitable ingredients for their dreys. In towns, where human litter is more common, they have been known to use plastic bags, drinking straws, and newspaper in the drey.

Gray squirrel drey cut in half to show inside

Life underground

PRAIRIE, PAMPAS, SAVANNA, STEPPE, and other types of grassland are some of the best areas to find burrowing mammals. As there are few trees, and so little shelter, the main refuge is underground. North American prairie dogs and ground squirrels, South American viscachas and maras, African root rats and mole-rats, and Asian sousliks and gerbils all tunnel in grasslands. They gain safety, a place to build a nest to rest and breed, and shelter from the hot sun and cold wind. But most of them have to emerge at some time, since they are chiefly herbivores, and plants do not grow underground in the dark. More specialized feeders, such as blind mole-rats, gnaw roots, bulbs, tubers, and other underground plant parts, and can stay permanently below the surface. Then there are the insect eaters, such as the moles.

BANKSIDE FRONT DOOR
The platypus retires to a burrow in the riverbank after feeding. Resting burrows are usually under tree roots, and are a few yards long. The breeding burrow is much longer, and as the pregnant female enters she blocks it with mud at intervals, to protect against floods and intruders and to keep herself warm. At its end, in a grass-lined nest, her eggs are laid (p. 31).

THE SNOW DEN
As the Arctic nights become almost continuous in winter, the mother polar bear digs a den in drifted snow. About one month later her cubs are born, and she stays with them and suckles them for around three more months. Spring arrives and the family emerges - cubs well fed and chubby, but mother thin and hungry, eager for her first seal meal for four months.

UNDER THE MOLE'S MOUND
Champion among mammal burrowers is the European mole, which lives, breeds, sleeps, and eats underground. A few mounds of fresh soil in a meadow are the only sign of a complex system of burrows and chambers 3 ft (1 m) or more beneath, and possibly stretching 300 ft (100 m) in length. The size of the burrow is determined largely by the richness of the soil. In old pasture, with lots of earthworms and insects, a mole would have to burrow less than in poorer, stonier, or sandier soil. Most of the food comes from the "mole patrol" as the animal wanders its tunnels, maintaining them and eating creatures that have fallen in from the walls.

KEY TO THE MOLE BURROW

1 The fortress - not an ordinary molehill, but the larger, more permanent mound above the mole's main nest

2 The nest - the female breeds in spring, giving birth to about four pink babies in a nest lined with grass, leaves, and other soft material

3 The mother mole - gathering nest lining is one reason for the mole's hazardous journeys aboveground, almost always at night

4 Surface run - some tunnels run just below the soil surface

5 Friend or foe? - European moles are solitary creatures. An individual that blunders into another's tunnels is usually chased away except in early spring when it could be a potential mate

6 The pantry - moles bite off worms' heads and store them in an underground larder, especially in autumn

7 Crisscrossing tunnels - these run at all angles

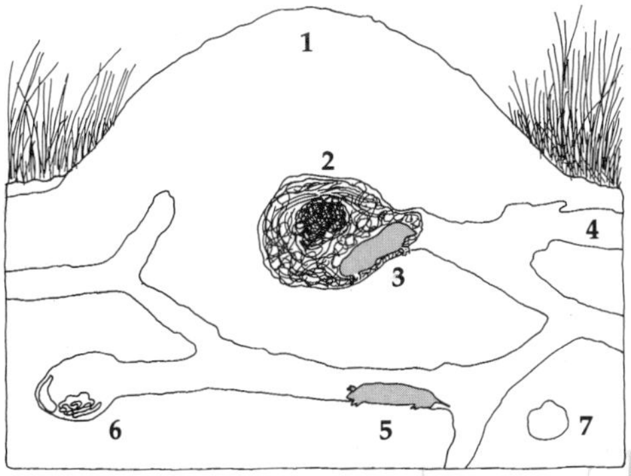

Key diagram

How many toes?

THE ORIGINAL MAMMALS probably walked on all four legs, on paws with five "fingers." Today there is almost every variation imaginable. The horse, a sizable mammal, walks on its tiptoes, and has only one toe on each foot. Small mammals such as the shrew still have all five digits. In general, a mammal with long limbs is a swift mover; short limbs indicate strength and perhaps digging ability. Gazelles and antelopes have ultraslim limbs for speed. Seals and bats possess large, finger-supported limb surfaces to push aside water or air. Claws, nails, hooves, fleshy pads, and other structures tip the toes.

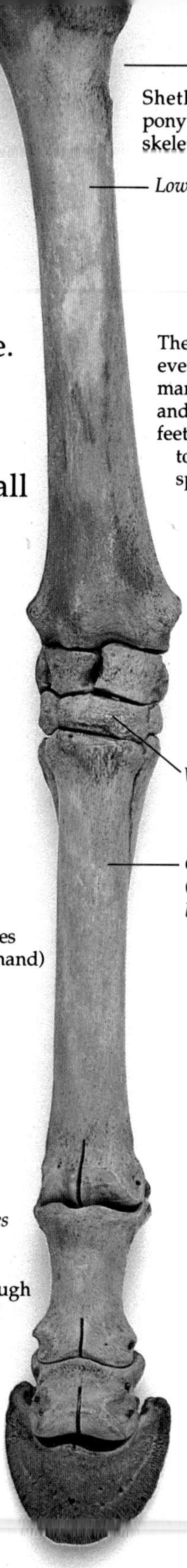

Shetland pony forelimb skeleton

Lower arm bone

Wrist bones

Cannon (palm) bone

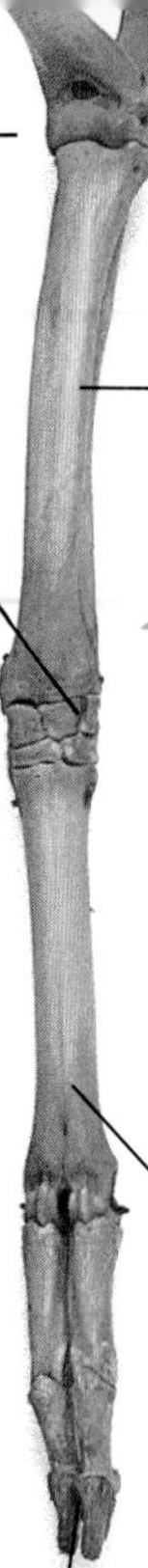

Soemmerring's gazelle forelimb skeleton

Lower arm bone

Wrist bones

Palm bone

Finger bones

TWO-TOED WALKING
The gazelles are even-toed hoofed mammals (p. 10), and these dainty feet allow them to run at great speed.

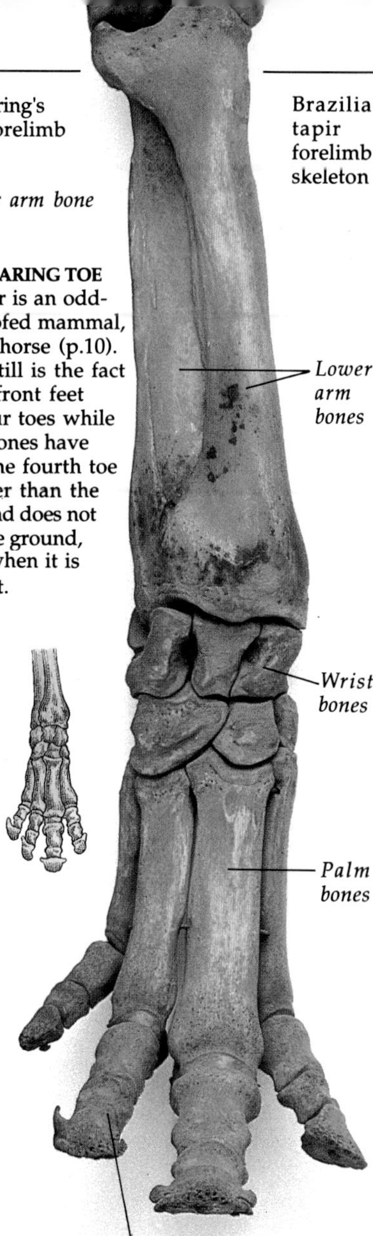

Brazilian tapir forelimb skeleton

Lower arm bones

Wrist bones

Palm bones

Finger bones

DISAPPEARING TOE
The tapir is an odd-toed hoofed mammal, like the horse (p.10). Odder still is the fact that its front feet have four toes while its back ones have three. The fourth toe is smaller than the others and does not touch the ground, except when it is very soft.

PENTADACTYL PLAN
The basic mammalian limb ends in five digits, like our own hands and feet. Many rodents, primates, and carnivores have kept this "pentadactyl" design. The hoofed mammals have lost different digits in different groups. Each bone, or set of bones, in the limb is represented by the same color throughout. (Names in brackets refer to the equivalent bones in the foot and lower leg.)

Key to colored bones (based on human hand)

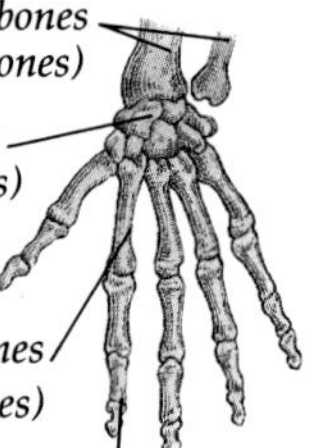

Lower arm bones (lower leg bones)

Wrist bones (ankle bones)

Palm bones (sole bones)

Finger bones (toe bones)

INSIDE THE HOOF
The zebra's hoof is made of hard, protective horn with a shock-absorbing pad of fat (the plantar cushion) between it and the toe bones.

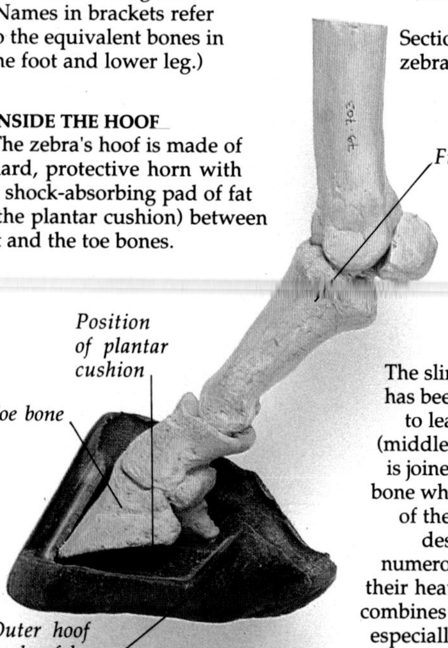

Section through zebra's hoof

Finger bone

Position of plantar cushion

Toe bone

Outer hoof made of horn

ONE-TOED WALKING
The slim limb bone of the horse has been modified by evolution to leave only one toe, the 3rd (middle) or pastern (p. 13). This is joined to a long, thick cannon bone which represents the fusing of the palm bones. The whole design does away with the numerous fingers and toes, with their heavy muscles and joints. It combines lightness with strength, especially toward the end of the limb, giving the horse its speed.

SAND-SHOED MAMMAL
The camel, another even-toed hoofed mammal, has enlarged, flexible foot pads that spread its weight well over the soft desert sand.

FLEXIBLE FEET
The dinky feet of the rock hyrax bear flattened nails, not true hooves: four at the front, three at the back.

CLAWS OF A KILLER
Sharp, retractable claws identify the owner of this skeleton as a member of the cat family - a domestic cat. The claws aid climbing and of course are used to slash at and hold down prey. Cats are "digitigrade," meaning they walk on their "finger-tips."

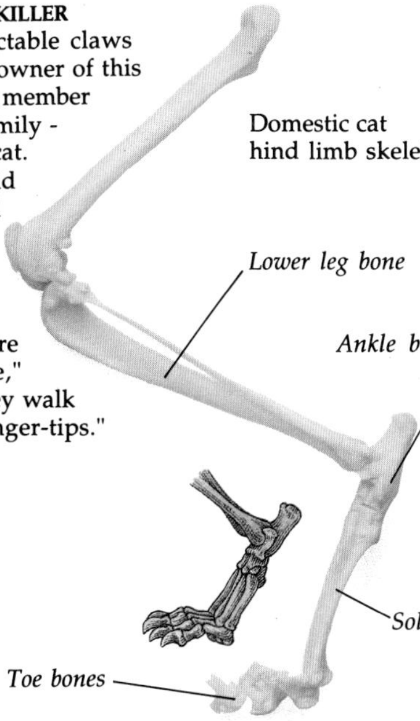

Domestic cat hind limb skeleton

BROAD-CLAWED DIGGER
Compared to the cat's limb, the European badger's leg is more powerful and thickset. The broad foot and wider claws are suited to digging and scratching, rather than the cat's slash. Badgers walk on their heels, and are known as plantigrade.

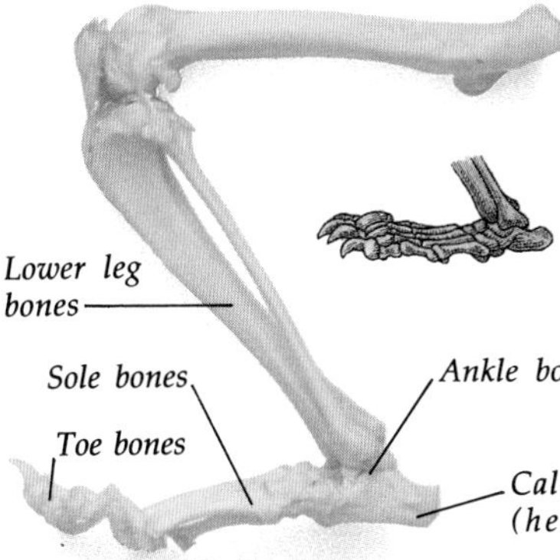

European badger hind limb skeleton

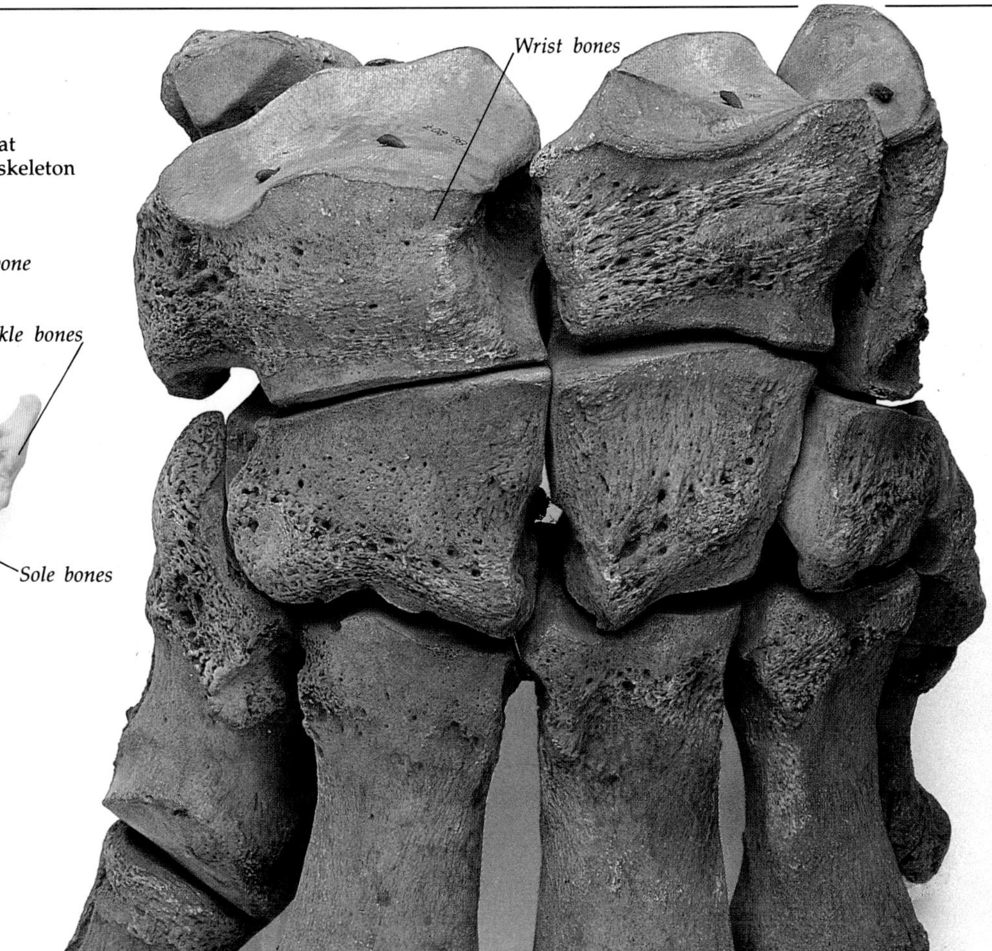

Elephant forefoot bones

THE GIANT'S FOOT
The enormous elephant needs enormous feet to carry its weight. A thick and flexible foot pad surrounds the toe bones and spreads the weight evenly over a large area (p. 61).

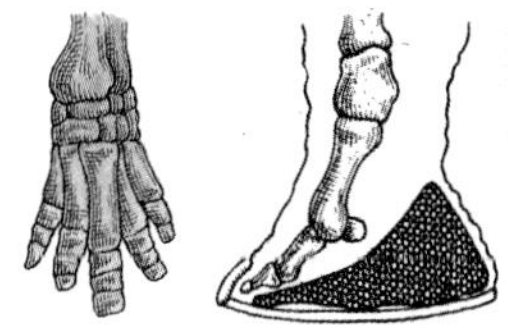
A fatty pad in the foot spreads the elephant's weight

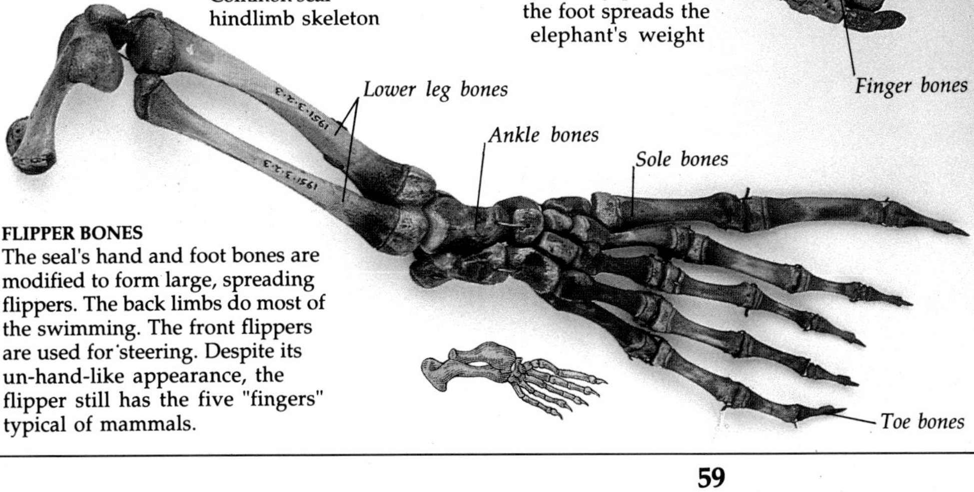

Common seal hindlimb skeleton

FLIPPER BONES
The seal's hand and foot bones are modified to form large, spreading flippers. The back limbs do most of the swimming. The front flippers are used for steering. Despite its un-hand-like appearance, the flipper still has the five "fingers" typical of mammals.

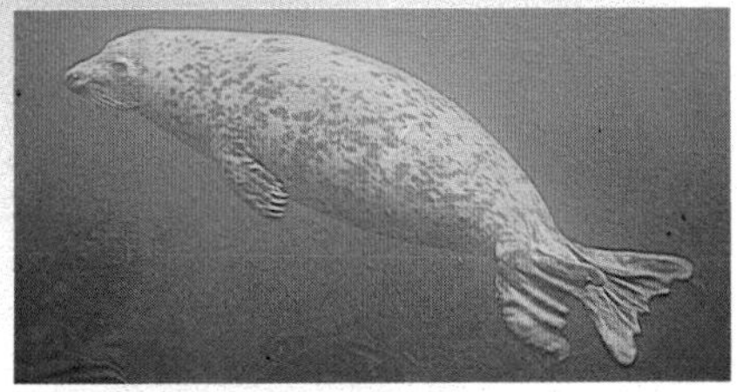
Gray seal using its flippers to swim

Badger footprints

Tracks and trails

Domestic cat

WALKING THROUGH any wild place, we are aware of many animals. Birds fly above, insects buzz from one flower to another, and fish rise to snatch food from the water's surface. But where are all the mammals? With their swift and active habits and their keen senses (p. 16) they make themselves scarce, fearing thc large creature blundering past. Others, being nocturnal, are well hidden and asleep. Although we are mammals ourselves, we seldom have the time and patience to glimpse our wild relatives. Often, we only know of their presence from the tracks and signs they leave behind; footprints and belly- or tail-drags in the ground, leftover bits of food with teeth marks, droppings, burrow entrances with dug-out soil, bits of hair caught on twigs and snagged on thorns, and castoffs such as antlers (p. 62). The footprints shown here are actual size, and actual prints made by the walkers themselves: real and messy, not cleaned and tidied up. The prints were made by encouraging the animals (by bribing with food) to walk on a pad of nontoxic ink and then across the paper. Claw marks do not show up using this technique, but they will be found in trails in soft mud or snow. In a trail, the spacing of the prints and the depths of their impressions allows us to work out whether the animal was running or walking.

Front print

Toe pad

Intermediate pad

Hind print

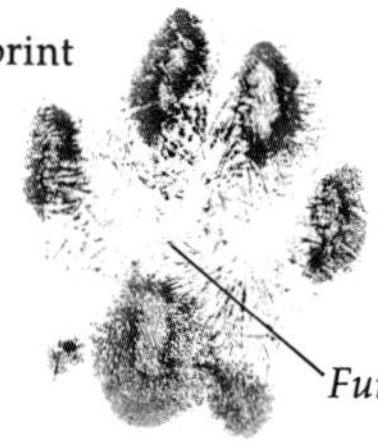

Fur on sole of foot

DIGITIGRADE KITTY
The domestic cat is digitigrade (a toe-walker, p. 59) and its toe pads are well separated from the main three-lobed sole, or intermediate pad. There are no claw marks: the claws are kept sharp in their sheaths until needed. Neither is there a mark from the innermost (1st) toe on each front foot, which is too high to leave a mark. Hence both front and hind prints are four-toed and roughly the same.

Front print

RUN, RABBIT, RUN
When sitting or hopping slowly, the rabbit's hind foot leaves its characteristic long imprint compared to the more circular front foot. But when running the difference is less obvious, since the animal tends to place only the tips of its hind feet on the ground.

Hind print

Feet are covered with fur - no pads show

Print of fur would not show up in snow

CLOVEN HOOVES
Animals that like mud provide plenty of prints in the soft ground. And the heavier the animal, the better. A half-ton wallowing buffalo left this clear cloven-hoofed print (divided in two), indicating it is an artiodactyl or even-toed hoofed mammal (p. 10).

Rabbit

Cat footprints

Rabbit footprints

Badger

Fore-print

Hind print

BIG FOOT
The distinctive imprint of the badger has five toe pads in a curved line above the main pad, although the inner toe is small and may leave only a small mark. These heavily built carnivores are plantigrade (p. 59) and usually leave good tracks. In its rolling walk, the badger's left and right limbs have a large gap or straddle between them.

LEAVING LITTLE IMPRESSION
Surprisingly, the heaviest land mammal, the elephant, often does not leave much of a mark with its feet. In soft ground there is a large, rounded print (above). But on looser, sandier soil the flexible foot pads (p. 59) spread the weight so effectively that prints are shallow or absent.

Hedgehog

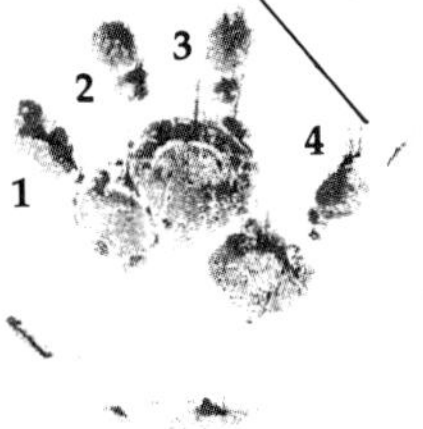

Front print

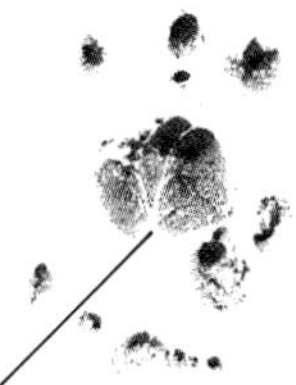

Hind print

MISSING BIG TOES?
The five-toed hedgehog usually leaves a four-toed track, because its inner (1st) toe is smaller and held farther from the ground. Like the badger, this stocky, plantigrade walker shows considerable straddle, with a gap of about 2 in (5 cm) between right and left feet. The toes of the front feet are more splayed (spread) than those on the back feet.

COMMON PRINTS: FOX OR DOG?
The red fox's prints can easily be mistaken for a dog's. Both of these carnivores are digitigrade, like the cat opposite. The fox's claws are usually visible and they are slightly longer and narrower than a dog's claws; also, the fox's toe pads are relatively smaller and more offset from center than in a dog. The hair between the pads shows clearly, and in winter it may grow so long that it obscures the pads and blurs the print's outline. As it trots, the fox puts each back paw in the print made by the front paw on that side of the body.

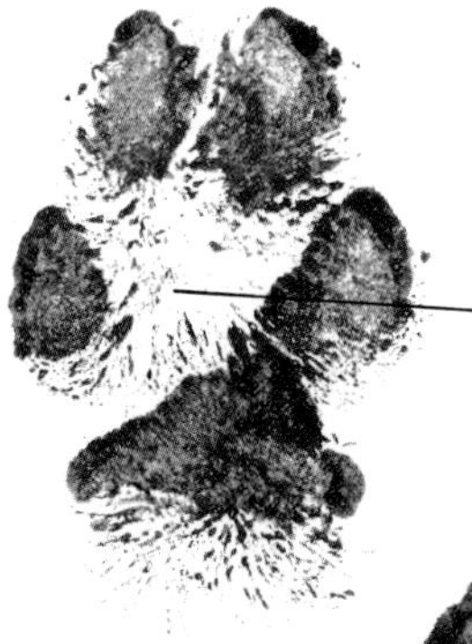

Front print

Hind print

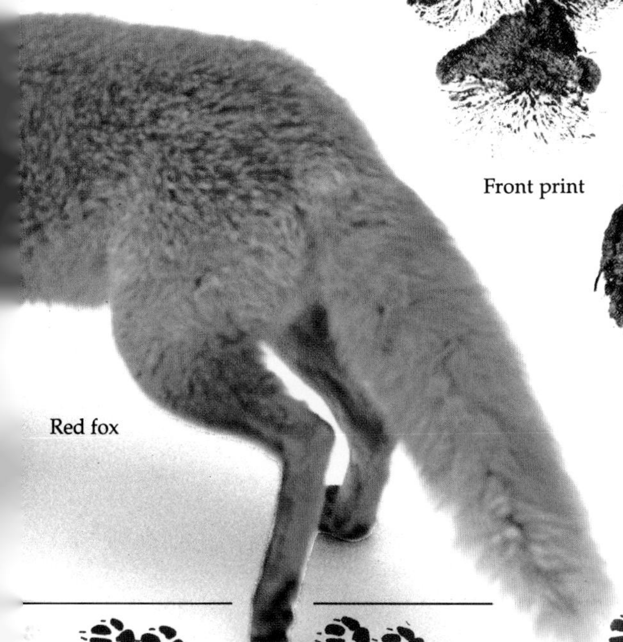
Red fox

ON THE TRAIL OF THE RAT
Rats and mice are small, light creatures and seldom leave distinct tracks, except perhaps in thin snow or in the dust on a shelf or granary floor. The toes are spread out and the claw points are sometimes visible. As in other mammals, the sole pads have sweat glands that leave tiny traces of sweat in the prints. Rats also leave greasy smear-marks along well-used trails in buildings.

Front print

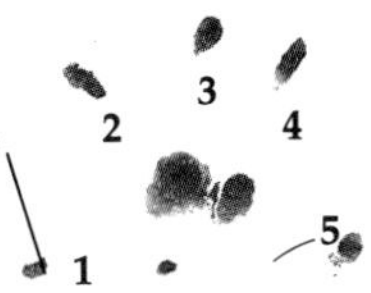

Hind print

Brown rat

Mammal detective

Indian trackers rely on their detective work for food

FOR MOST PEOPLE TODAY, contact with the natural world is limited to the garden or park, or an occasional walk in the woods. This unfamiliarity with nature breeds a type of blindness: when out on a walk we look, but we don't know exactly what for. Yet there are still groups of peoples around the world who live with nature, in the manner of our ancestors. We can only wonder at their knowledge and experience when it comes to "detective work." The merest hint of gnawing or a dropping is quickly identified since it is important - it could lead to meat for food, bones for tools, and skins for clothes and shelter. Yet anyone can learn. It's a question of having the time and needing the knowledge.

Long-lasting bones

Bones, teeth, horns, antlers, and other hard parts of the mammal body tend to persist long after the flesh and soft organs have been eaten or rotted away. To the trained eye, a crack or dent in a certain place can indicate the manner of death. Wear on the teeth may show that the owner was old and weak and perhaps died from disease.

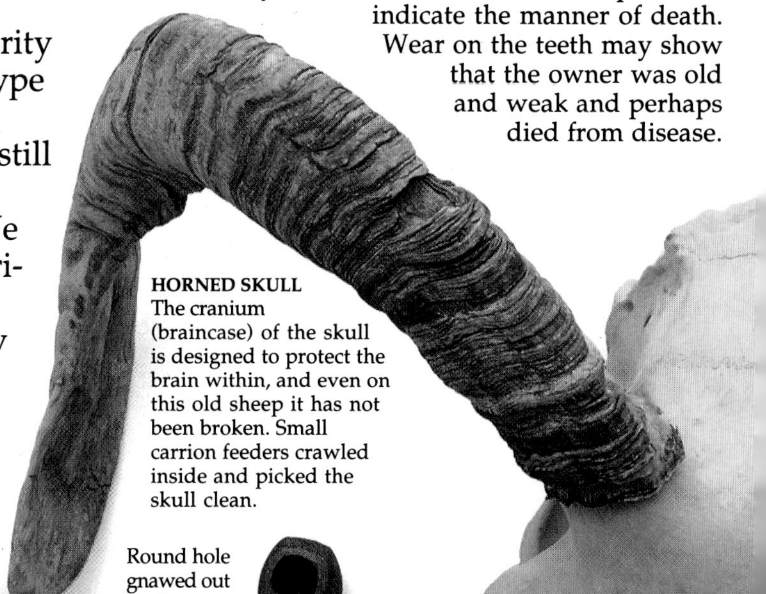

HORNED SKULL
The cranium (braincase) of the skull is designed to protect the brain within, and even on this old sheep it has not been broken. Small carrion feeders crawled inside and picked the skull clean.

Fascinating dung

Many mammals have regular defecation stations, and the droppings are often used as territorial markers, as when an otter leaves its spraints, or feces.

Rabbit droppings

RABBIT "PEAS"
Rabbits use their droppings to scent-mark territory.

SQUIRREL SIGNS
Squirrels strip the scales from pine cones to reach the nutritious seeds sandwiched inside.

Squirrel-gnawed pine cones

Round hole gnawed out by dormouse

Nut split cleanly in two by adult squirrel

NUTCRACKERS
The hard shell of the hazelnut is a challenge, but the delicious kernel inside is worth it. Different mammals tackle the shell in characteristic ways.

Irregular hole in side, the work of a yellow-necked mouse

Teeth at work

Rodents are the champion gnawers. Even when not feeding, they gnaw experimentally at many different materials using their chisel-shaped incisor teeth (p. 50).

Shells gnawed by rat

SNAILS UNSHELLED
A brown rat on the beach neatly gnawed these snail shells to eat the occupants.

Roe deer droppings

DEER DROPPINGS
Deer eat lots of low-nutrient food and so leave large amounts of droppings.

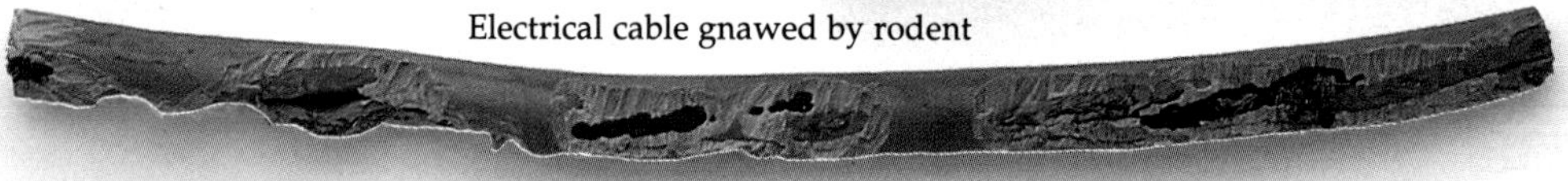

Electrical cable gnawed by rodent

POWER CUTS
Rats and mice may gnaw at electrical cables to find out what is inside. This can have consequences. Sometimes the animal is electrocuted. Fires and power cuts have been started by such "innocent" rodent behavior.

Lower jaw of gnawing animal - long incisors

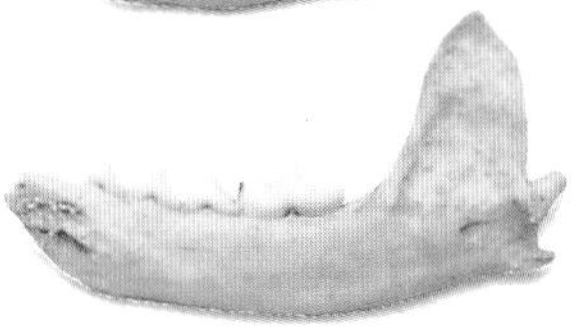

Lower jaw of carnivore - carnassial tooth

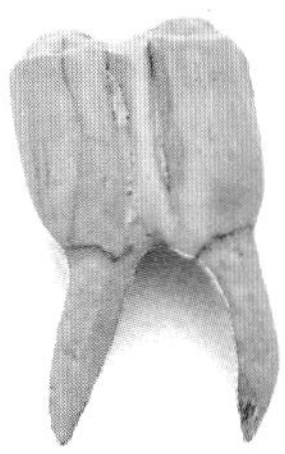

Herbivore's tooth - flat, grinding top

BLEACHED, BEACHED BACKBONE
Cleaned white by the sea, this fur seal's vertebra (backbone) was washed up on the appropriately named Skeleton Coast, Namibia, (South-West Africa). The salty water has caused chemical corrosion, dissolving out the weaker substances to show the internal structure of bone.

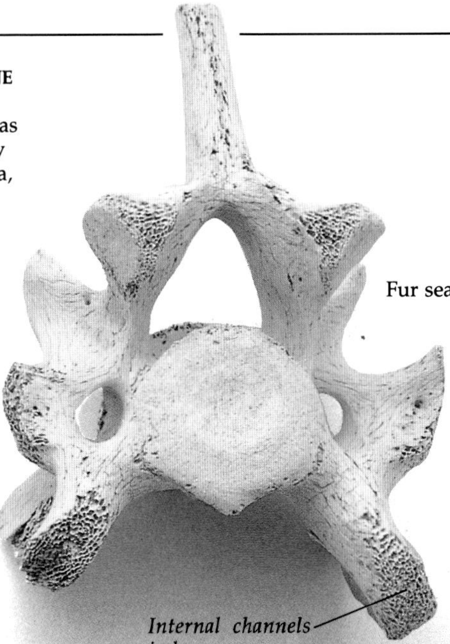

Fur seal vertebra

UNREWARDING MOUTHFULS
Jaws and teeth are rarely eaten by a predator, since the teeth are too hard and their roots project into the jawbone.

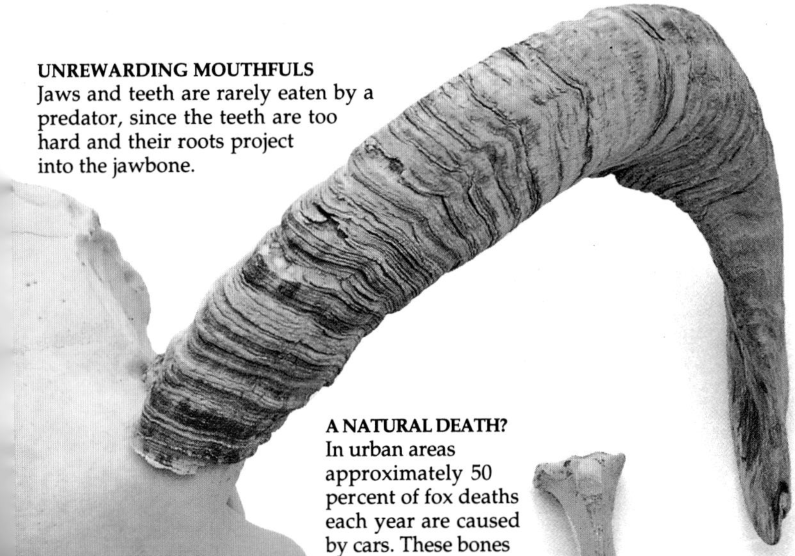

A NATURAL DEATH?
In urban areas approximately 50 percent of fox deaths each year are caused by cars. These bones were found near a main road. Perhaps the fox was hit by a car and crawled away before dying.

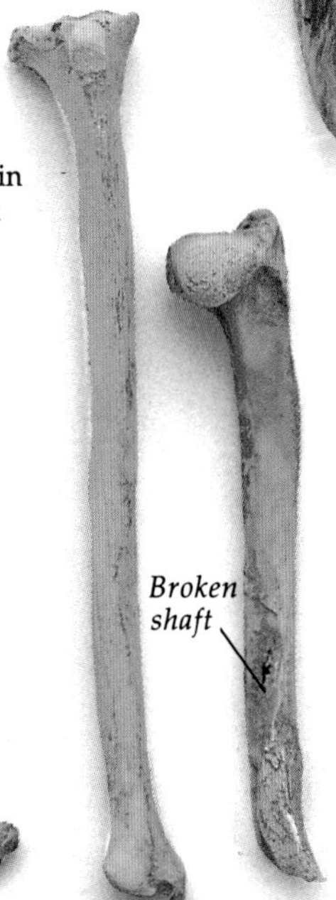

Limb bones

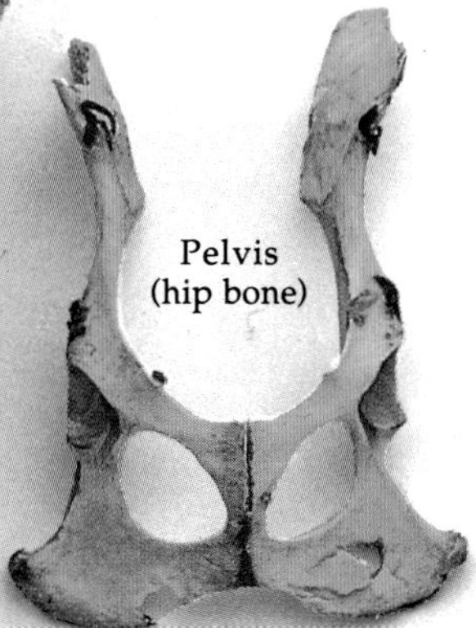

Pelvis (hip bone)

CASTAWAY
Deer lose or cast their antlers each year and grow a new set. The roebuck uses its antlers in duels with other males (p. 26) and also rubs them on trees during the summer to mark his territory.

A PILE OF WINGS
This indicates that a bat is nearby. They are partial to the juicy bodies of moths, but allow the dry wings to drop into a neat heap below their roost.

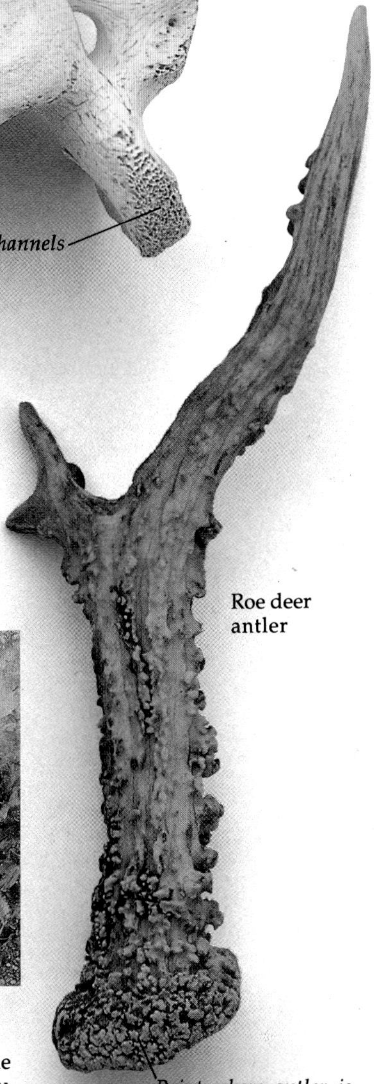

Roe deer antler

Furs on the fence

Barbed wire is the artificial equivalent of the thicket, and just as good at snagging fur from passing animals. The height at which the fur was caught, and the size of the hole through which the animal pushed, are important clues, as well as the color and nature of the hairs.

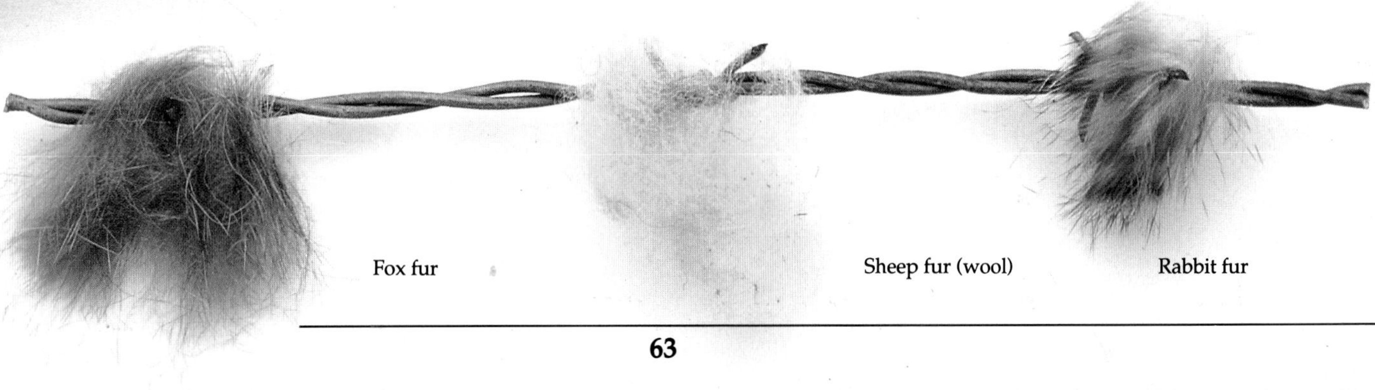

Fox fur

Sheep fur (wool)

Rabbit fur

Did you know?

AMAZING FACTS

Across the world, humans are the most widely distributed mammals, closely followed by the house mouse (*Mus musculus*), which has accompanied humans to all parts of the world.

On average, a newborn kangaroo is only 1 in (2.5 cm) in length.

The first mammals began to evolve around 200 million years ago. Early mammals were small insect eaters, rather similar to the modern shrew. At the time, dinosaurs dominated the Earth. Mammals were able to survive because their warm-blooded nature meant that they could be active at night when it was safer to hunt for food.

Common shrew

The first-known zoo was created in China by the emperor of the Chou Dynasty in about 1100 BCE.

The armadillo and the pangolin are the only mammals to have reptile-like scales instead of fur.

An adult lion's roar can be heard up to 5 miles (8 km) away and can either frighten off intruders or reunite a pride of lions that has been scattered.

Bats are the only mammals that can fly.

The most prolific breeder among mammals is the North American meadow vole (*Microtus pennsylvanicus*), which can produce 17 litters in a single year, at an average of six or seven babies per litter.

The farthest distance migrated annually by any sea mammal is the 12,427 miles (20,000 km) traveled by the gray whale. It makes the journey from its breeding grounds in Mexico to its summer feeding grounds in the Bering Sea.

Among the 233 species of primate, body size can vary greatly. An adult male gorilla can weigh as much as 452 lb (205 kg), while the tiny pygmy marmoset (*Cebuella pygmaea*) weighs in at just 5 oz (140 g) for the average male.

At night, dolphins rest just below the surface of the water, but keep moving.

Tigers are the only big cats that are striped all over.

A rat can last longer without water than a camel can.

The fastest land mammal is the cheetah, which can run at speeds of up to 62 mph (100 k/ph), but only in short bursts. The pronghorn antelope (*Antilocapra americana*) can maintain a speed of 31 mph (50 k/ph) over a distance of several miles.

A sperm whale can eat 1 ton of squid daily

The blue whale (*Balaenoptera musculus*) is the largest of all mammals, in fact, all animals, that have ever lived. Measuring up to 110 ft (33.5 m) long and weighing up to 147 tons (150 tonnes), its heart alone is the size of a small car, and 50 humans could stand on its tongue. The sperm whale has the biggest head of any living creature on land or in the sea. It is also the only animal with a gullet big enough to fit a human.

All pet hamsters are descended from a single female wild golden hamster found with a litter of 12 young in Syria in 1930.

Domestic cats are the only species of cat able to hold their tails vertically while walking. Wild cats carry their tales either horizontally or tucked between their legs when on the move.

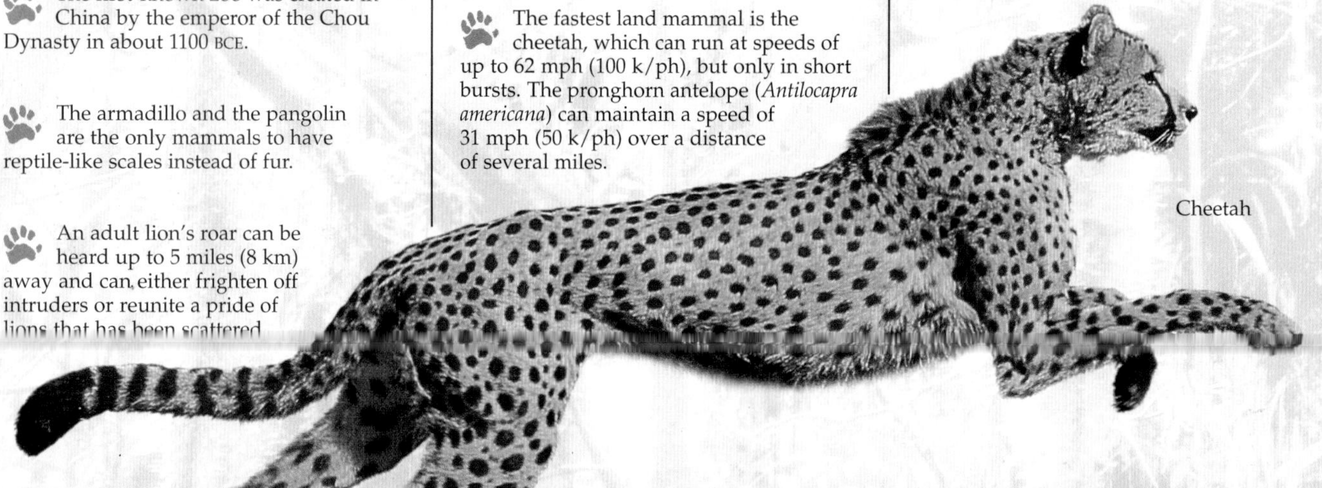

Cheetah

QUESTIONS AND ANSWERS

Record Breakers

SMALLEST LAND MAMMAL

• The record is a close call between the Kitti's hognosed bat (*Craseonycteris thonglongyai*), which is about 1 in (2.54 cm) long and 0.06 oz (1.6 g) in weight, and the pygmy shrew (*Suncus etruscus*), which averages about 1.5 in (3.8 cm) in length and weighs 0.05 oz (1.5 g).

HEAVIEST BRAIN

• The sperm whale has the heaviest brain of any living animal. At about 20 lb (9 kg), this whale's brain is four times heavier than a human's.

SMALLEST SEA MAMMAL

• The smallest sea mammal is Commerson's dolphin (*Cephalorhynchus commersonii*), which averages 4.1 ft (1.25 m) in length and weighs 522 lb (237 kg).

LONGEST LIFESPAN

• Humans are the longest-lived mammals, but the Asian elephant comes a close second, with the oldest known specimen having lived to 78.

Q Which mammal has the longest gestation period?

A The Asiatic elephant (*Elephas maximus*) has the longest gestation period at 22 months. Opossums have the shortest pregnancy of any mammal, and bear their young just 12–13 days after conception.

Q Which mammal is the deepest sea diver?

A The sperm whale can dive the deepest, at 1.8 miles (3 km). Northern elephant seals (*Mirounga angustirostris*) can dive to depths of 0.9 miles (1.5 km).

A pair of Northern elephant seals

Q Can a mammal ever be cold-blooded?

A A mammal is by definition a warm-blooded creature. However, there are some interesting exceptions to this rule. The naked mole-rat (*Heterocephalus glaber*)—which lives on the desert fringes of Somalia, Ethiopia, and Kenya—cannot maintain a steady body temperature. Its temperature fluctuates with that of the atmosphere, making this creature essentially cold-blooded. Naked mole rats huddle together to slow their rate of heat loss and bask in shallow tunnels warmed by the sun. The Arctic ground squirrel (*Spermophilus parryii*) is also unusual in that it is the only mammal that can lower its body temperature to just below freezing during hibernation. By doing this, the squirrel saves energy, which helps it survive the Arctic climate.

Q What is the biggest land mammal?

A The biggest land mammal is the African bush elephant (*Loxodonta africana*). Adult males can measure up to 11 ft (3.3 m) in length and weigh up to 6.8 tons (7 tonnes).

African bush elephant

Arctic ground squirrel, native to Alaska

Q Which mammal has the biggest eyes?

A The tarsier is one of the smallest primates and lives in the forests of Borneo and Sumatra in the Philippines. A tarsier averages 6 in (15 cm) in length, but its eyes are proportionally so large that they would be equivalent to grapefruit-sized eyes in a human. Galagos, known as bush babies, also share the tarsier's large eye-to-body ratio. They can be found in sub-Saharan African forests.

Mammal classification

THERE ARE 19 groups of classification for mammals. Each group, called an order, is shown here with one example illustrated. Some orders contain hundreds of species, while others only have one. The way mammals are classified changes all the time as scientists discover more about the evolution of mammals and their relationships with each other.

Elephant

PROBOSCIDEA
There are only two species of proboscidea alive today: the Indian elephant (*Elephas maximus*) and the African elephant (*Loxodonta africana*). The now extinct mammoth once belonged to this group. Elephants are rare in that they live by a female-led social structure.

Kangaroo

Most kangaroos cannot walk, but hop using their hind legs.

MARSUPIALIA
Traditionally, marsupials are classified in a single order, but some scientists think that they should be divided into seven. Four of these orders are native to Australia and neighboring islands, while the other three are found in North and South America. Marsupials carry their young in an abdominal pouch called a marsupium.

Platypus

MONOTREMATA
Monotremes include three species of egg-laying mammals: the platypus and two species of echidna, or spiny anteaters. Monotremes are only found in Australia, Tasmania, and New Guinea. Monotreme species have not altered significantly in the past two million years.

Hyrax

HYRACOIDEA
Although they resemble rodents or rabbits externally, hyracoid, or hyraxes, are actually ungulates, or hoofed mammals. This links them to groups such as horses, although they also share characteristics with groups such as elephants, sea cows, and aardvarks! There are seven species of hyrax.

Seal

PINNIPEDIA
Pinnipedia comes from the Latin for "fin footed" and covers 33 species of seals, sea lions and fur seals, and walruses. Pinnipeds spend the majority of their lives in water and have bodies that are adapted to move easily through an aquatic habitat. They cannot move very well on land.

Dermoptera means "skin-wing."

Colugo

DERMOPTERA
This group contains the colugos, with just two species, both from Southeast Asia. Sometimes called flying lemurs because they resemble lemurs, colugos do not fly, but rather glide on flaps of skin. Colugos are herbivores and have very sharp teeth.

INSECTIVORA
Members of this order feed mostly on insects and tend to be small. Numbering around 375 species, this group includes hedgehogs, moles, and shrews. Insectivores have well developed hearing, smell, and touch, rather than vision. They are found everywhere except Australia.

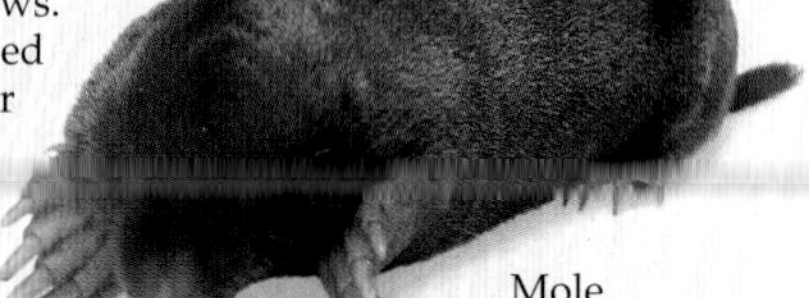

Mole

Gerbil

RODENTIA
Rodents have a pair of front teeth that continue to grow throughout life. They use these teeth to gnaw through their food, and through anything in their way. Rats, squirrels, hamster, mice, and gerbils are all rodents.

Fox

CARNIVORA
Most carnivores are meat-eating land mammals. They can be recognized by their teeth, which are shaped for grasping flesh and slicing it up. Carnivores tend to be medium-sized animals with excellent senses. Numbering around 270 species, carnivores include foxes, dogs, cats, wolves, and bears.

CHIROPTERA
This group includes bats, the only mammals capable of powered flight. Bats have poor vision and rely on echolocation, or hearing, for navigation. They emerge only at night to hunt for food. Making up one quarter of all mammals, there are 1,000 species of bats.

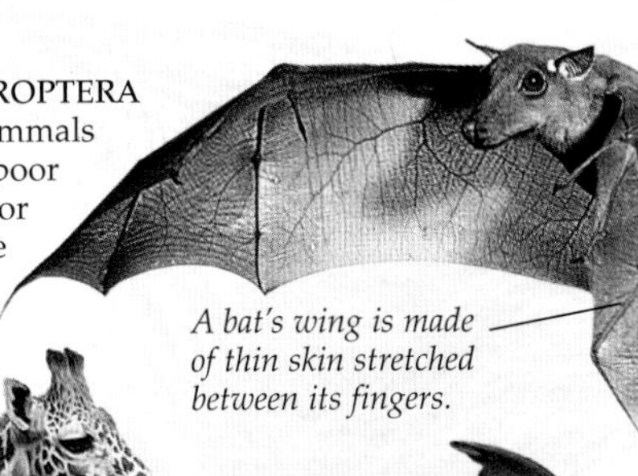

A bat's wing is made of thin skin stretched between its fingers.

Bat

Sloth

A sloth lives hanging upside down

EDENTATA
Edentata means "without teeth," but only some members of this group—anteaters—have no teeth at all. The other members, sloths and armadillos, have rootless molars. Edentatas are found only in the Americas. Pangolins used to belong to this group but now belong to a separate classification.

Giraffe

Subspecies of giraffe can be distinguished by their coat patterns.

With its long legs and neck, the giraffe is the tallest of all land animals.

Dolphin

CETACEA
There are 78 species of whales, dolphins, and porpoises in this group. Much study has been undertaken of the behavior of cetaceans, which often display playful characteristics as well as signs of remarkable intelligence.

ARTIODACTYLA
This large and diverse group contains around 220 species. Artiodactyla means "even-toed" and refers to the number of digits on each foot, which is usually two, but sometimes four. Pigs, giraffes, and hippopotamuses all belong to this group.

Aardvark

TUBULIDENTATA
The only member of this order is the aardvark. This hairy, nocturnal creature eats ants and termites. It uses its large claws to dig up insect nests and then sticks its long tongue into the nest to get to its prey. Aardvarks also use smell and hearing to seek out nests.

Rabbit

LAGOMORPHA
Lagomorphs cover about 80 species of rabbits and hares. They have a fast reproductive rate and most females can produce many litters of young in one year. Like rodents, they have long incisor teeth which continue growing throughout life.

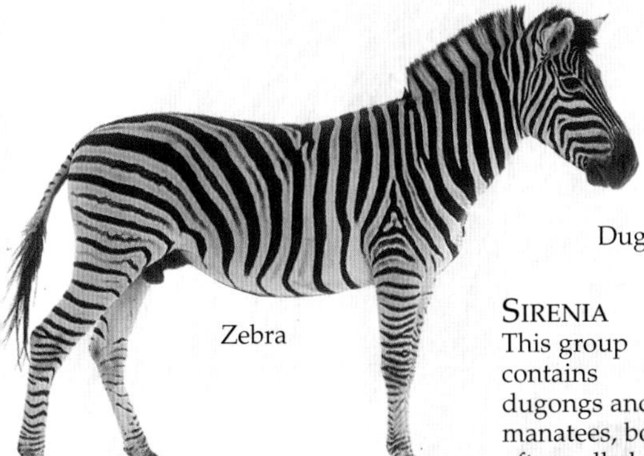

Zebra

PERISSODACTYLA
This group is made up of hoofed mammals that have an odd number of toes. Like most artiodactyls, they walk on their hooves rather than their feet. There are 17 species of perissodactyls, including rhinoceroses, horses, zebras, and tapirs. Most members are herbivores.

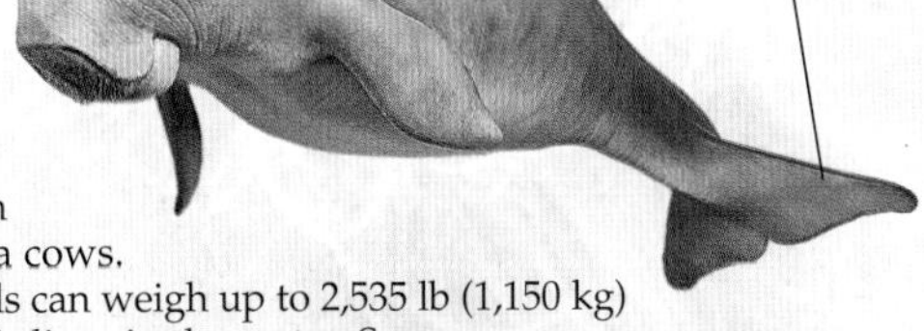

Dugong

The dugong has a tail instead of hind flippers.

SIRENIA
This group contains dugongs and manatees, both often called sea cows. These mammals can weigh up to 2,535 lb (1,150 kg) and spend their lives in the water. Sea cows are endangered because they are hunted for meat.

PRIMATE
There are about 180 primate species, one of which is humans. Primates tend to have long limbs and flexible fingers and toes. They also have wide, forward-facing eyes and larger brains than other animals of the same size.

Chimpanzee

PHOLIDOTA
Pangolins were once classified as edentates, but now occupy a group all by themselves. Also known as scaly anteaters, pangolins have many rows of overlapping scales that protect the body. They have no teeth but a long tongue.

Pangolin

Find out more

TO LEARN MORE ABOUT mammals, you can start right at home. Many households often have at least one pet, and, more often than not, this will be a mammal. Don't forget that humans are mammals too, so with family and friends, you will never be short of primates to observe! A trip to a farm shows how mammals are bred and kept in communities. To study exotic species, visit a zoo, aquarium, or wildlife park, and to learn about the history of mammal evolution check out your nearest natural history museum. A walk in the country may reveal some mammals—but not the shy ones!

USEFUL WEB SITES

- Enchanted Learning: All about mammals
  www.enchantedlearning.com/subjects/mammals/
- University of California Museum of Paleontology: Hall of Mammals
  www.ucmp.berkeley.edu/mammal/mammal.html
- Monterey Bay Aquarium: Marine Mammals in the Wild
  www.mbayaq.org/efc/efc_fo/fo_mammal.asp
- National Museum of Natural History, Smithsonian Institution
  www.nmnh.si.edu/vert/mammals/mammals.html

A DAY AT THE ZOO
Most major cities have a zoo containing animal species from around the world. Zoos are important to conservation because they allow endangered species to be bred in captivity when conditions in the wild threaten their extinction. These species can then be reintroduced to the wild, where their numbers can increase again. Zoos give people a chance to study animals that they would not usually get to see, such as the camels above. In the past, zoo animals were sometimes kept in cramped conditions, but modern zoos try to give animals plenty of space.

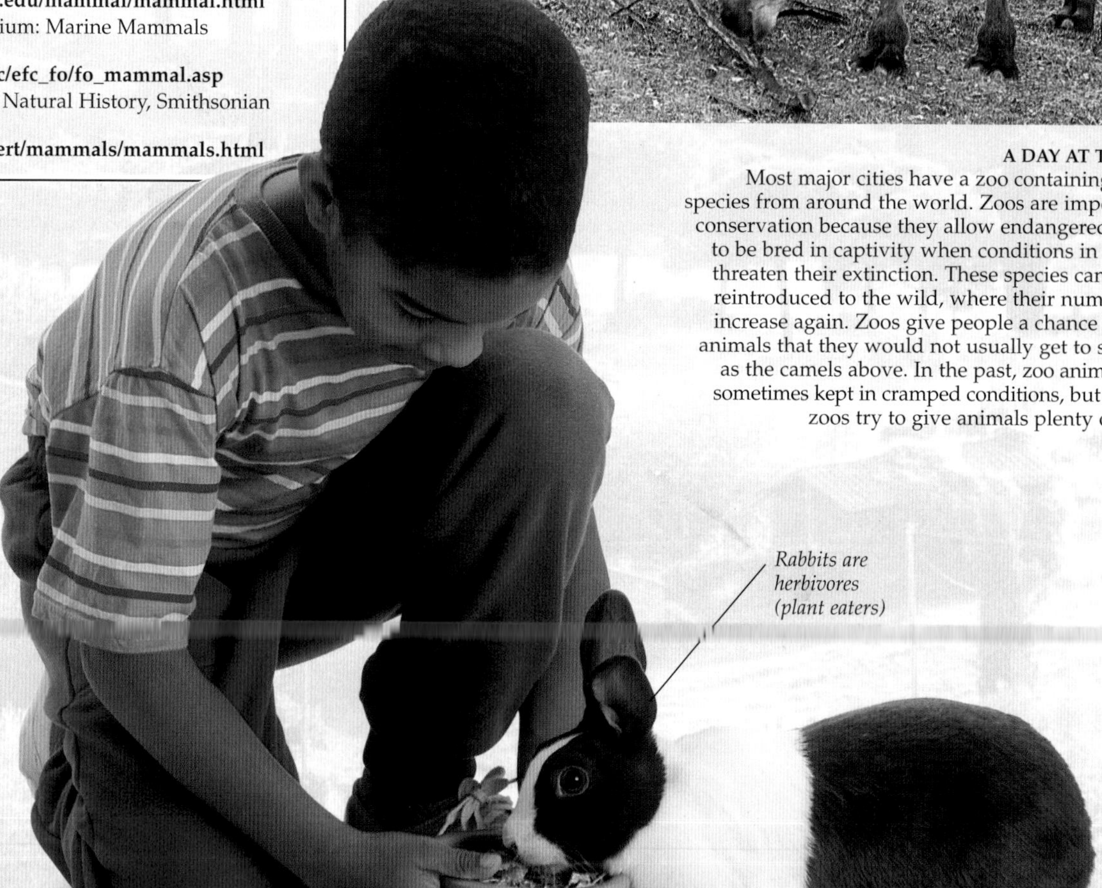

Rabbits are herbivores (plant eaters)

PETS AT HOME
Cats, dogs, gerbils, mice, rabbits, and many other common pet choices are all mammals. Studying your pet can teach you a great deal. Find out your pet's species name, which classification order it belongs to, and how it compares to other members of its order.

Visitors are not allowed to leave the vehicle for their own safety.

GO WILD ON SAFARI
A "safari" originally meant a hunting or viewing trip to see animals in the wild in Africa. Today there are safari parks all over the world. These are vast enclosures that allow animals to wander around in relative freedom. Although the animals are kept in separate reserves, or zones, to keep them from hunting each other, these conditions resemble the wild much more closely than a zoo. Visitors can drive through the reserves in the protection of a vehicle and view lions, tigers, elephants, and many other species up close.

DOWN ON THE FARM
Some farms are open for tours, and some cities now have a farm for people who cannot visit the countryside frequently. On a farm you can see many mammals, such as sheep, cows, pigs, and horses. In these communities you can watch mammals feeding their young, grazing for food, and interacting with each other.

Places to Visit

SAN DIEGO ZOO, SAN DIEGO, CALIFORNIA
www.sandiegozoo.com
Thousands of animals live in this zoo and wild animal park. Highlights include a children's zoo, Panda Central, the Polar Bear Plunge, and Absolutely Apes.

BRONX ZOO, BRONX, NEW YORK
www.bronxzoo.com
This terrific zoo includes Congo Gorilla Forest, the Himalayan Highlands Habitat (with snow leopards), and an indoor Asian rain forest covering almost an acre.

HOUSTON ZOO, HOUSTON, TEXAS
www.houstonzoo.com
The Houston Zoo is home to more than 100 species of mammals. Visitors can see exhibits such as the Wortham World of Primates, Carnivores, Hoofrun, and Natural Wonders, an area featuring storytellers and hands-on demonstrations.

PURINA FARMS, GRAY SUMMIT, MISSOURI
www.purina.com/company/profile/purinafarms.asp
Visitors can pet dogs and cats or milk a cow at this interactive farm.

Binoculars allow good views of animals without disturbing them.

NATURE WATCH
Take a trip to your local nature reserve or countryside, accompanied by an adult. Set up in a quiet spot and silently observe the wildlife around you. You may be lucky enough to see mammals such as squirrels, badgers, or deer on the move.

Glossary

AMNIOTIC MEMBRANE A thin membrane that surrounds a developing embryo inside its mother's uterus, or womb

ARTIODACTYL A hoofed mammal that has an even number of toes on each foot, usually two, but sometimes four. Deer, camels, and sheep all fall into this group.

BALEEN PLATES The fringed plates that hang from the roof of the mouth of the largest types of whale. Baleen plates filter small animals from sea water for food.

CAMOUFLAGE The means by which an animal escapes the notice of predators, usually because it blends in with its surroundings

CARNIVORE An animal that eats meat

CARTILAGE A gristly substance in the body of animals. In some animals it forms the whole skeleton. In others it forms the coverings of the bones in a joint, and the framework of parts such as the ears.

CELL A microscopic unit that is the building block of most living things

CHORDATE The main group of vertebrates (animals with a backbone)

CLASSIFICATION A way of grouping living things to show how they are related

CLOVEN Hooves divided into two parts in certain mammals, such as pigs and deer

COLONY A number of related living things that live closely together

DETRIVORE An animal that eats the remains of dead animals, plants, and other living things

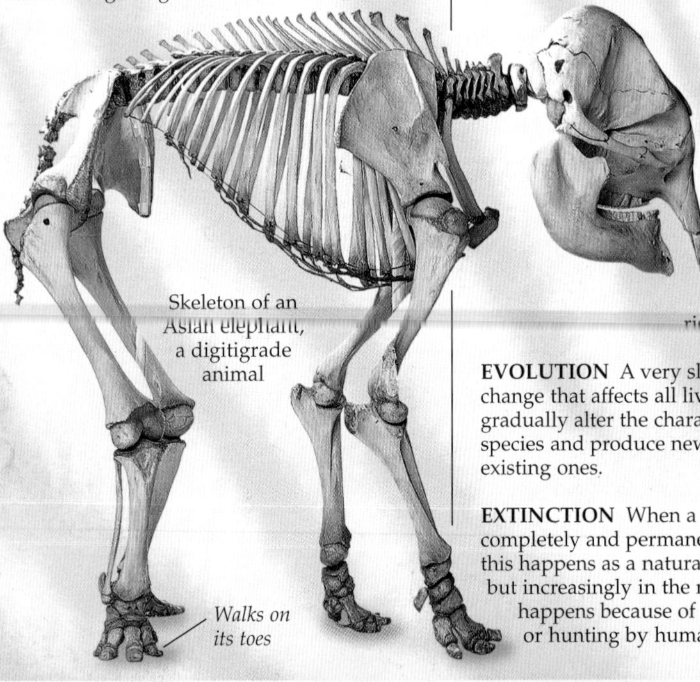

Skeleton of an Asian elephant, a digitigrade animal

The giant panda is an endangered species

DIGESTION The breakdown of food into nutrients, tiny parts small enough to be absorbed into the body. In most animals, digestion takes place in a tube that runs through the body.

DIGITIGRADE An animal which walks only on its toes and not the flat surface of its foot

DNA This is the abbreviation for deoxyribonucleic acid, the chemical that carries all the information needed to build a living thing and keep it alive. DNA is passed from one generation to the next when living things reproduce.

ECHOLOCATION A way of sensing objects by using high-pitched sounds. Bats, dolphins, and some whales use echolocation to "see" in the dark or in water.

ECOLOGY The study of the relationship between living things and their environment

EMBRYO The early stage of development of an animal or plant

ENDANGERED A species whose numbers have decreased so much that they are at risk of extinction

EVOLUTION A very slow process of change that affects all living things. It can gradually alter the characteristics of a living species and produce new species from existing ones.

EXTINCTION When a species dies out completely and permanently. Sometimes this happens as a natural result of evolution, but increasingly in the modern world it happens because of pollution or hunting by humans.

FETUS An unborn mammal in the later stages of development

FOOD CHAIN A food pathway that links different species in a community, passing down energy and nutrients from one organism to another. Each species is usually involved in several different food chains. The amount of energy passed on decreases at each stage.

FOSSIL The remains or traces of a living thing preserved in rock

GENE The basic unit of heredity. Genes are passed from parents to offspring and determine each living thing's characteristics. Most genes are made of DNA.

GESTATION The period of time that a baby spends growing in its mother's womb before it is born

A white rhinoceros has a gestation period of 16 months.

GRAMINIVORE An animal that eats mainly grains, seeds, nuts, and similar tough plant materials and fibers

GRAZE To eat vegetation, usually grass or other low-lying plants

GUARD HAIR The outside layer of a mammal's fur that protects the inner fur and the skin from wet weather conditions

HABITAT The environment needed by a particular species for survival

HERBIVORE An animal that eats mainly plant material, especially leaves, buds, shoots, fruits and stems, and flowers

HIBERNATION A sleep-like state experienced during winter by many small animals. During hibernation, the animal's body enters a state of torpor, which means that its body temperature drops and its metabolism slows down.

INSECTIVORE An animal that eats mainly insects

Red-necked wallaby, a marsupial

INSTINCT A pattern of behavior that occurs naturally in an animal and does not need to be learned

JOEY A baby kangaroo or wallaby

KRILL Tiny sea-dwelling organisms eaten by whales, seals, and fish

LIFE CYCLE The pattern of changes that occurs in each generation of a species

MAMMAL A warm-blooded animal with fur that feeds its young on milk

MAMMARY GLAND The milk-producing organ of a female mammal

MARSUPIAL A mammal that develops inside its mother's pouch, such as a kangaroo or a wallaby

MATING The coming together of a male and female animal during sexual reproduction

METABOLISM All the chemical processes that take place in a living thing

MIGRATION A regular journey made by an animal from one place to another, often timed according to the seasons

MONOTREME A mammal that lays eggs, such as a duck-billed platypus or a spiny anteater

A spiny anteater is a monotreme

MOLTING The process of shedding hair or fur

MUSCLE A tissue in the body that contracts to produce movement

NERVE A bundle of specialized cells that carry signals rapidly around the body of an animal

NERVOUS SYSTEM The network of nerve cells in an animal's body, including the brain

NOCTURNAL An animal that is active at night and inactive during the day

OFFSPRING The young or descendants of an animal

OMNIVORE An animal that eats any kind of food, whether of plant, animal, or fungal origins

OVARY An organ in a female animal that produces egg cells

PENTADACTYL An animal with five toes or fingers. Humans are pentadactyls.

PHEROMONE A chemical released by one animal that has an effect upon another. Pheromones may be released to mark a trail, warn off intruders, or attract a mate.

PLANTIGRADE An animal that places the full length of its foot on the ground during each stride when walking

PISCIVORE An animal that eats mainly fish

PLACENTA An organ which develops inside the womb during pregnancy and which passes oxygen and food from the mother's blood to the blood of the fetus

PREDATOR An animal that hunts other animals

PREY The animals that are hunted and eaten by a predator

PRIMATE A mammal with flexible fingers and toes and forward-pointing eyes. Humans are primates.

REPRODUCTION The production of offspring

RODENT A mammal with sharp incisor teeth used for gnawing. Rats, mice, and squirrels are all rodents.

SEX CELL A special cell used during reproduction

SKELETON The supporting framework of an animal's body that is usually jointed to allow movement

SPECIES A group of living things whose members can breed successfully with each other to produce fertile offspring, but who cannot breed with any other living things

SUCKLING A baby animal that still feeds on its mother's milk

SYMBIOSIS An interaction between two living organisms living in close physical association

TERRITORY An area claimed by an animal

UNGULATE A hoofed mammal

VEGETATION The plants that grow in a particular habitat

VERTEBRATE An animal with a backbone. There are five main groups of vertebrates: fish, amphibians, reptiles, birds, and mammals.

WARM-BLOODED When an animal can make its own heat by burning up food. It can be warm even when its surroundings are cold. One of the key characteristics of a mammal is that it is warm-blooded.

The gorilla is the largest of all primates.

Index

Acknowledgments

The publisher would like to thank:
Jane Burton and Kim Taylor for all their ideas, hard work and enthusiasm.
Dave King and Jonathan Buckley for additional live animal photography.
Daphne Hills, Alan Gentry, and Kim Bryan at the Natural History Museum for the loan of the specimens and for checking the text, and Colin Keates for photographing the collections.
Hudson's Bay, London, for loan of furs.
Will Long and Richard Davies of Oxford Scientific Films for photographing the section through the molehill.
Jo Spector and Jack.
Intellectual Animals, Molly Badham, and Nick and Diane Mawby for loaning animals.
Elizabeth Eyres, Victoria Sorzano, Anna Walsh, Angela Murphy, Meryl Silbert, and Bruce Coleman Ltd.
Radius Graphics for artwork.
David Burnie for consultancy.

Picture credits
t = top; b = bottom; m = middle; l = left; r = right

Archive for Kunst und Geshichte, Berlin: 12b; 15b
Pete Atkinson/Seaphot: 59b
Jen and Des Bartlett/Bruce Coleman Ltd: 29b
G I Bernard: 37bl; 60m
Liz and Tony Bomford/Survival Anglia: 33t
Danny Bryantowich: 23bl
Jane Burton: 27m
Jane Burton/Bruce Coleman Ltd: 17b; 18b; 21mr; 27t; 34b; 36b; 46t; 53m;
John Cancalosi/Bruce Coleman Ltd: 27m
Sarah Cook/Bruce Coleman Ltd: 64b
Peter Davey/Bruce Coleman Ltd: 49bm
Wendy Dennis/FLPA – Images of nature: 67b
Jeff Foott/Bruce Coleman Ltd: 39t
Frank Greenaway: 63m
David T. Grewcock/Frank Lane Picture Agency: 53tm
D Gulin/Dembinsky/FLPA – Images of nature: 65tr
David Hosking/FLPA – Images of nature: 64cl, 67c
Johnny Johnson/Bruce Coleman Ltd: 65br
Zig Leszczynski/Oxford Scientific Films: 48m
Will Long and Richard Davies/Oxford Scientific Films Ltd: 57
Mansell Collection: 19t
Mary Evans Pic. Library: 8tl; 16bm; 20m; 26m; 28m; 29m; 31m; 37bl; 46b; 49br; 58m
Richard Matthews/Seaphot: 27t
Military Archive & Research Services Lincs.: 22b
Minden Pictures/FLPA – Images of nature: 64tr, 65bl, 71br
Stan Osolinski/Oxford Scientific Films Ltd: 44t
Richard Packwood/Oxford Scientific Films Ltd: 16br
J E Palins/Oxford Scientific Films Ltd: 16bl
Dieter and Mary Plage/Bruce Coleman Ltd: 61r
Dr Ivan Polunin/NHPA: 66bl
Masood Qureshi/Bruce Coleman Ltd: 45b
Hans Reinhard: 26m
Jonathan Scott/Planet Earth: 53mt
Sunset/FLPA – Images of nature: 70t
Kim Taylor/Bruce Coleman Ltd: 32b
University Museum of Oxford: 70bl
Martin Withers/FLPA – Images of nature: 66c, 69t
Jacket images:
Front: Daniel Heuclin/NHPA, b
Back: Natural History Museum, bl

Illustrations by John Woodcock:
8; 9; 10; 11; 13; 14; 19; 20; 27; 58; 59

AFRICA
AMERICAN REVOLUTION
AMPHIBIAN
ANCIENT CHINA
ANCIENT EGYPT
ANCIENT GREECE
ANCIENT ROME
ARCHEOLOGY
ARCTIC & ANTARCTIC
ARMS & ARMOR
ASTRONOMY
AZTEC, INCA & MAYA
BASEBALL
BASKETBALL
BATTLE
BIBLE LANDS
BIRD
BOAT
BOOK
BUDDHISM
BUILDING
BUTTERFLY & MOTH
CAR
CASTLE
CAT
CHEMISTRY
CHINA
CHRISTIANITY
CIVIL WAR
CLIMATE CHANGE
COSTUME
COWBOY
CRIME & DETECTION
CRYSTAL & GEM
DANCE
DA VINCI & HIS TIMES
DESERT
DINOSAUR
DOG
EAGLE & BIRDS OF PREY
EARLY HUMANS
EARTH
ECOLOGY
ECONOMY
ELECTRICITY
ELECTRONICS
ELEPHANT
ENERGY
EPIDEMIC
EVEREST
EVOLUTION
EXPLORER
FARM
FILM
FIRST LADIES
FISH
FLAG
FLYING MACHINE
FOOD
FOOTBALL
FORCE & MOTION
FORENSIC SCIENCE
FOSSIL
FUTURE
GORILLA, MONKEY & APE
GOYA
GREAT MUSICIANS
GREAT SCIENTISTS
HORSE
HUMAN BODY
HURRICANE & TORNADO
IMPRESSIONISM
INDIA
INSECT
INVENTION
ISLAM
JUDAISM
JUNGLE
KNIGHT
LIFE
LIGHT
MAMMAL
MANET
MARS
MATTER
MEDIA & COMMUNICATION
MEDICINE
MEDIEVAL LIFE
MESOPOTAMIA
MONET